Gourmet Gifts from Your Kitchen

Gourmet Gifts from Your Kitchen

Ceil Dyer

MACMILLAN PUBLISHING CO., INC.
New York

COLLIER MACMILLAN PUBLISHERS
London

Jacket from an original painting by Prentiss Kent

Line Drawings by Carl Smith

Our thanks to the Sugar Association, Inc. for the use of their recipes.

Macmillan Publishing Co., Inc.
866 Third Avenue, New York, N. Y. 10022
Collier-Macmillan Canada Ltd.

Library of Congress Cataloging in Publication Data

Dyer, Ceil.

   Gourmet gifts from your kitchen.
    1. Cookery (Fruit) 2. Confectionery. 3. Baking.
4. Gifts. I. Title.
TX811.D9   641.8   73-14425
ISBN 0-02-534510-9

First Printing 1974
Printed in the United States of America

Contents

Introduction

Today, when most people buy their jams and jellies, cookies, cakes, candies and such at a supermarket, anything homemade is a special treat. Yet preserving, baking, and candy-making is so easy, so much fun to do, and so rewarding. Though any present you make yourself is a special compliment, because so few people have time to make their own, something delicious to eat is especially welcome.

This book contains my own collection of recipes suitable for gift-giving. Begged and borrowed over the years from good cooks and gift-giving friends, these recipes with the flavor of home are all special, unique, and unbuyable.

There are old-fashioned fresh fruit jams and jellies, elegant conserves, honest marmalades, epicurean chutneys, and some very special spiced and brandied fruits. Cakes for any number of occasions and cookies to suit every taste are included. There are rich but not-so-sweet tea breads and coffee cakes. And, of course, there's a chapter on candies—from Christmas candy canes; the recipe is from Maine—to sophisticated California bars of natural fruits and nuts. Lastly,

because every gift list contains a difficulty or two—
dieters who recoil with horror at the thought of sugar,
those few souls who don't really like sweets, rich girls
who have everything and bachelors who rarely eat at
home—there is a chapter I call "This and That"
which includes mostly nonsweets: a cheese spread
spiced with fine brandy and packed in a stoneware
crock, old-time bread and butter pickles, my best and
most successful relish, a few very fine flavored vinegars,
and a lemon butter that is honestly the best I ever ate.

Even if you've been cooking for a long time, I think
you will find throughout the book both new and old
(but forgotten) recipes that you will enjoy making and
which will enrich your repertoire and enhance your
reputation. However, even if you have not as yet
boiled your first egg, if you follow instructions and
read the "how to" at the beginning of each chapter
you literally can't fail to please your family and friends
—as well as be pleased yourself—with your results.

Gift-cooking is happy cooking—creative and
pleasurable. I hope you feel as I do about it. When I
walk into the kitchen I can't wait to begin.

Happy giving.

"Of Shoes
-and Ships-and
Sealing-Wax"

—With apologies to Lewis Carroll

Wrapping and Shipping Your Gifts

The most attractive jars for jellies, jams, and preserves
are just plain mason jars with their old-fashioned
homey charm. Simple handwritten labels do nicely,
but if you go in for jelly- and jam-making in a big
way, you might like to have your own labels printed.
I have had labels designed for as little as $10 by a
student in our local art school. My labels had a sketch
of my house and there was space for me to write in
the type of jam, jelly, or preserve. Just be sure your
design looks attractive in black and white. Printing a

one-color label is not expensive, but start adding colors and the price skyrockets.

There are all sorts of ways to gift-wrap and decorate your jars, but here's my favorite, which is also the easiest: Take a square of gift paper 3 times as wide as the jar is tall; for example, if the jar is 4 inches tall (half-pint), you will need a 12-x-12-inch square of paper. Place the jar on its side about 1 inch from the edge of the paper and roll up. Fold the smaller end neatly under the jar and fasten with tape. Now gather the top of the paper over the jar and tie tightly with ribbon or cord. The paper "collar" will stand up in a gay "ruff" on the top of the jar. You can go on to decorate as fancifully as you like, but I think they look best with just gift paper and ribbon. Here are a few combinations I've found effective:

Paisley-print paper with gold cord (especially good for chutney)
Shiny white paper with olive-green velvet ribbon
Brown and white bookbinding paper with brown velvet ribbon
Pink and white checked "gingham" paper with red grosgrain ribbon (nice for apple jelly)
Silver paper with white grosgrain ribbon
Black and white checked paper with red yarn
Plain old-fashioned brown wrapping paper with wide red or green velvet ribbon
Gold paper with brown twine instead of ribbon
Strawberry print paper with grass-green ribbon (for strawberry jam)
Bright green paper with bright green ribbon (for mint jelly)
Red-flocked "Victorian" paper with dark-green velvet ribbon

There are endless combinations, of course. I know of one girl who even wrapped her jars in newspaper and tied them with red velvet. The point is to try for a fresh look that's all your own.

If you are planning to mail anything packed in breakable jars or bottles, there are certain tricks to packing that need to be learned if they are going to arrive intact. First, you need a generous-sized box. The basic idea in packing breakables is to have them tightly nested in enough shredded paper to keep them from coming in contact with a hard surface if the package is dropped or bounced about, and I guarantee

it will be, no matter how many large red "fragile" labels you may paste on it. I've found it best to have the shipping box at least 4 times the size of your jars or bottles.

Fill the box half full of shredded newspaper, pack it in tightly, then wrap each piece in a "sleeve" of corrugated paper or, even better, a piece of the marvelous new plastic "bubble" wrap. This is sometimes available in stationery stores. If not, you can usually get the shipping department of a local department store to sell you some. I used to get mine at Bloomingdale's in their "central wrap" deep in the basement.

Wrap each item snugly in its protective sleeve, fasten with tape, and place at least 3 inches apart in the bed of shredded paper. Pack in as much shredded paper as the box will hold, and I do mean pack it in tightly, making sure the contents cannot possibly move. Next, seal the box securely with professional sealing tape. (I use Scotch Brand Package Sealing Tape.) Paste on at least 2 "fragile" labels, address it, and off it goes.

In packing cakes, cookies, and candies, the same rules for shipping breakables apply. Naturally, you are not going to try to ship iced or delicate cakes or fragile crisp cookies. These are "takables" only, but solid cakes such as pound and applesauce or fruitcakes ship very well if carefully packed. I like to seal cakes first in a plastic bag then wrap in aluminum foil. The only further decoration needed is a handsome bow of appropriate ribbon. Velvet is especially pretty against the foil; 1-inch wide ribbon seems to make the most effective bow.

The cake is then slipped into a sleeve of corrugated paper or bubble wrap. Again, be sure your cake is nested securely in plenty of shredded paper in a

6

generous-sized sturdy box, taped firmly and addressed clearly.

Solid cookies such as date-nut bars and creamy candies such as fudge and penuche travel best. Wrap first in plastic wrap, then stack in a gift box. Plain white ones from the variety store do nicely. I like to wrap the box in foil to help keep the contents fresh, and rely on good-looking ribbon for decoration. There's a good reason for this. Elaborate wrapping is all too likely to get crushed in shipping and the package emerges looking not gay but sloppy.

Two mailing tips: First, be sure to include zip codes for both send and return addresses; they save days in delivery time. Second, I've found air parcel post to be not much more expensive than regular mail and it's much faster. Also, because air mail gets preferential treatment, there is less chance of your package being banged about.

To make it easy and simple to gift-wrap and ship your "wares," see if you can set up a cabinet or closet to hold all your supplies near a handy counter where you can work. Here's a checklist for the things you will need.

Scissors
Cellophane tape
Assorted gift papers
Assorted ribbons and cords
Gift cards with ties
Aluminum
Plastic bags
Two or three different sizes of shipping cartons
    (these can be purchased flat and easily assembled
    when you are ready to ship a package)
Package-sealing tape

Twine (necessary on overseas or registered)
"Fragile" labels
Address labels (optional)
Zip code book
Heavy marking pen for addressing
Bathroom scale (optional, see below)

In most cities in the United States there is a marvelous shipping service called United Parcel. Check your telephone book for their number. United Parcel delivers in almost every city and town in the country and they are fast, reliable, and cheap. Moreover, for a small fee (usually about $2) they will come and pick up your package, which is a godsend, especially if you don't drive, or the weather and traffic are both impossible, or you have a number of heavy packages to get off. UPS, as they are known, is much less expensive than parcel post and usually as fast as air mail. The only catch is you must call them a day in advance and be prepared to give them the size, weight (there's that need for a scale), and contents of each package. You must also have the zip code numbers. Packages may be insured for any amount, and the fees are low. Insurance up to $100 is free. The person who takes your order will figure the total amount and give it to you. You have only to make out a check and give it to the driver, who will give you a receipt. It's a super-convenient service, in my opinion.

Once you get started giving your friends your home-made creations, you will probably never give anything else. It's also habit-forming for the recipient. People are easily spoiled by real honest-to-goodness jams, jellies, and preserves, cookies, cakes, candies and such, so be prepared to keep it up. No one is going to be happy with a commercial gift from you next year.

All About the Preserving Arts

All the recipes here are easy to prepare, but if this is your first adventure in preserving, here's the most successful way to go about it.

Have the proper equipment. Most of the necessary utensils will doubtless already be in your kitchen, but do invest the small amount required to have everything you need. Once you begin preserving for gift-giving, chances are it will become a yearly pleasure and well worth the small outlay for materials.

Have everything ready and lined up before you start. Then give the cooking procedure your undivided attention. During the few minutes you leave the room, your jam may get too thick or the fruit butter may scorch.

Use very good fruit. You can't make fine preserves

with poor-quality fruit. Think in terms of economy by purchasing what is abundant and low in cost rather than by buying fruit not at peak freshness.

Equipment

Large, heavy kettle: Kettle must have enough surface area for mixture to cook down properly, must be high enough so contents won't boil over when the bubbling begins, must be heavy enough so contents won't scorch.

Large ladle: for filling jars with finished products.

Accurate measuring cups and spoons

Sharp knives: for chopping and paring

Blender, food mill, or grinder: for pureeing fruits.

Cheesecloth: for straining juices for jelly, for bundling spices

Large colander or strainer: for washing fruits and straining juices

Clock with a second hand: for timing commercial pectin jellies

Containers: jelly jars, canning jars, jelly glasses

Paraffin: for sealing jelly glasses

Labels: for marking the jar contents and preparation date

Candy or jelly thermometer: This is not essential —I rarely use one—but it does take out all guesswork in determining the exact amount of doneness, particularly when making jelly.

Tests for Doneness

There are three tests for determining if preserves have been cooked long enough. The temperature and refrigerator tests may be used for both jelly and jam and other preserves; the spoon or sheet test is for jelly.

Temperature test: Check the temperature of boiling water with a jelly, candy, or deep-fat thermometer. The temperature at which water boils differs at different altitudes and may change with atmospheric conditions. For jelly, cook the jelly mixture to a temperature of 8°F. above the boiling point. For jam and other preserves, cook the mixture 9°F. above the boiling point, taking care to stir thoroughly just before reading the thermometer.

Refrigerator test: Remove the jam or jelly mixture from the heat. Pour a small amount of the boiling mixture onto a chilled plate. Put the plate in the freezer compartment of the refrigerator for a few minutes. For jelly, the mixture has cooked sufficiently if it has jelled. For jam, if only a small amount of liquid runs away from the mound of jam, it is thick enough.

Spoon or sheet test: Dip a cold metal spoon in the boiling jelly mixture. Lift the spoon out so that the syrup runs off the side. When the drops run together and fall off the spoon in a sheet, the jelly is done.

Jars and Sealing

The best containers for all preserves are vacuum-sealing jelly jars and small canning jars. Jellies and smooth jams may be stored in jelly glasses sealed with paraffin, but paraffin seals sometimes loosen and are not recommended for long storage periods. If jellies are to be used quickly, they can be put in whatever jars are on hand. But for long storage and more professional results, bona fide jelly jars that produce a vacuum seal are best.

Using Self-Sealing Jars

Make certain the rims are free of nicks that might admit air. Make sure your lids are fresh. Discard any worn ones and worn rubber linings as well. Wash the jars, lids, and bands in hot soapy water. About 15 minutes before the end of cooking time, remove the jars, lids, and bands from the soapy water and rinse well in scalding water. Invert in dish drainer or drain on a towel, keeping well away from drafts.

Preserves must be boiling to produce a vacuum seal. Ladle the mixture into a jar, holding the ladle close to the top of the jar to keep air bubbles from forming. Fill to within ¼ inch of the top. With a damp cloth, wipe the rim and threads of the jar. Place lid on jar with rubber sealing part next to the jar. Screw the band on evenly and tightly. Invert the jar for a few seconds so that the hot mixture can destroy any mold or yeast on the lid. Then stand the jar upright to cool.

Fill and seal one jar at a time. Don't attempt an assembly-line procedure.

As the jam cools, a vacuum is formed in the jar. The pop you hear coming from the kitchen after you've finished means that a vacuum has been formed and that the jar is truly sealed.

After the jelly or jam has completely cooled, test the seal by pressing the top of the lid. If it is firm, the seal is good. If you can depress the lid, a vacuum has failed to form; use this jar first. Or place any jars that haven't sealed on a rack in a pan; cover with boiling water. Boil for 10 to 15 minutes to "can" the contents and produce a seal.

Using Jelly Glasses

Proceed as above for washing and rinsing jelly jars. Fill the glasses with boiling jelly to within ¼ inch of the top, holding the ladle close to the edge as you pour to prevent air bubbles. Cover the jelly immediately with ⅛ inch of melted paraffin. For a good seal, the paraffin must touch the sides of the glass all the way around. With a wooden pick, prick any air bubbles around the edge of the paraffin or elsewhere. Allow glasses to stand undisturbed until the paraffin hardens and then cover with loose-fitting lids.

Storage of Jams and Jellies

Jams and jellies keep best in a cool, dark, dry place. Since they represent considerable work and care, be sure to store well.

Preserving is such a satisfactory art. It's simple and fun to do and the results can add infinite variety to every meal you serve. Jams and jellies, conserves, marmalades, and such are not only an addition to the breakfast table but can and should be used to spark luncheons and dinners as well.

To Speak of Jams

"The rule is, jam tomorrow and jam yesterday—but never jam *today*."

"It *must* come sometimes to 'jam today,'" Alice objected.

"No, it can't," said the Queen. "It's jam every *other* day: today isn't any *other* day, you know."

Lewis Carroll
Through the Looking Glass

Despite the royal logic, queens, like commoners, can often be mistaken. Any other day can be today if we decree it, and we can indeed have jam today—strawberry, cherry, peach, plum, or any other if we chose the proper day for making.

When roadside stands and supermarkets offer fruits in abundance and at bargain prices, why then the perfect other day has come. It's the day to give yesterday and tomorrow to other less joyful things and now, right now, enjoy the pleasures of jamming. The fragrance of fresh fruit and its beauty, the sounds of the bubbling kettle, and the taste—ah, the taste—there is nothing that quite comes up to the taste of fresh homemade jam—spread on hot-from-the-oven breakfast rolls, spooned over ice cream, used in an authentic English trifle or in any number of other splendiferous concoctions.

Though certainly very nice jams are to be found on supermarket shelves, there is simply no comparison in taste, texture, and color to "homemade." Even the most expensive gourmet jam is not its equal.

Great jams can be made only in small batches, and this is impossible for even the best commercial makers. For them the other day can never be, but for you and

15

for me it's ours for the taking—to prove to Alice that the day does come, not just sometimes but often, for jam and its making and giving.

Old-Fashioned Blackberry Jam

3 quarts blackberries
Sugar
2 tablespoons lemon juice

Dump berries in a large pan of water. Swish them around and then lift them out, leaving sand and dirt in the bottom of the pan. Mash and measure. To each cup mashed berries add ¾ cup sugar.

Combine berries, sugar, and lemon juice in the preserving kettle and stir over low heat until sugar dissolves. Increase heat and let boil hard to jelling point. Stir frequently to prevent sticking. Skim surface.

Ladle boiling hot into clean hot jars. Seal.

Makes 7 to 8 half-pint jars.

Note: This same recipe can be used to make any berry jam.

Banana Jam

3 quarts sliced medium-ripe bananas (about 12 large bananas)
6 cups sugar
1½ cups orange juice
¾ cup lemon juice

Combine all the ingredients in a large kettle. Stir over moderate heat until sugar dissolves. Boil rapidly for 10 minutes, then reduce heat and simmer, stirring frequently, until thickened, about 15 minutes. (The banana slices break up as they cook, making a smooth jam.) When jam is thick, remove from heat, ladle immediately into clean hot jars, and seal.

Makes 9 to 10 half-pint jars.

Banana-Orange Jam

2 tablespoons lemon peel
3 large lemons
8 large oranges
3 pounds bananas
6 cups sugar

Grate the lemon peel and set aside.

Peel all the lemons and 6 of the oranges, then slice them as thinly as possible, discarding seeds. Squeeze the juice from the remaining oranges. Peel and cut the bananas into thin slices.

Combine all the ingredients in the preserving kettle and stir over low heat until the sugar has dissolved. Increase heat and let simmer for about 45 minutes or until very thick. Stir occasionally at first, then as the mixture thickens, stir almost constantly.

Ladle into clean hot jars and seal.

Makes about 6 half-pint jars.

Old Timey Blueberry Jam

If you can obtain blueberries that are only half ripe—deep red instead of blue—the resulting jam will be spectacular, sweet but tart and of a beautiful color, with a taste similar to the elegant lingonberry preserve found only in Scandinavia.

1 quart underripe blueberries
4 cups sugar
½ cup water

Wash the berries and discard any that are green or overripe.

Spread the sugar out on a baking sheet and place it in a warm (150°F.) oven.

Place the berries in a large enamel or stainless steel preserving pot and mash them with a wire potato masher. Then add the water and bring slowly to the boiling point over very moderate heat. Let boil gently for about 20 minutes or until soft, then add the warmed sugar. Adjust the heat upward and cook the mixture rapidly until the liquid reaches the jelling point. As it thickens, stir often to prevent sticking.

Test for doneness: remove kettle from heat, put a little of the jam on a cold plate, and place in the freezing compartment of your refrigerator; if it holds its shape it is ready.

Skim the surface quickly, then ladle while still boiling hot into clean hot jars. Seal.

Makes 3 to 4 half-pint jars.

Cherry Currant Jam

This is really a superb jam. The cherries remain plump and whole with the flavor of just-picked fruit.

1 quart not very ripe currants
2 pounds tart red cherries
4½ cups sugar
½ cup water

Pick over the currants, discarding any that are bruised or damaged, but don't stem them. Place them in a colander and wash under cold running water. Drain, then put them in a large heavy pot. With a potato masher or a heavy wooden spoon, mash the currants until the juices flow. Then place over moderate heat and cook them until soft and mushy. Strain the juices through a fine sieve lined with a clean cloth. For a beautiful crystal-clear jelly with plump cherries suspended throughout, use a flannel cloth and don't—no matter what—squeeze or mash the fruit. Just let the juice drip through at its own pace. This can take several hours, so the best strategy is to leave it overnight. Next morning the juice will be ready and you can continue.

First pit the cherries. This is not really a hard job; just use a small sharp knife and work over a bowl to catch all the juices.

When the cherries are pitted, pour the cherry juice over the sugar in the preserving pot and add the water. Place over low heat until sugar dissolves, then bring to a boil and boil about 5 minutes. Add the currant juice and the cherries and boil gently until the juices sheet from the spoon so that you know you will have a firm jelly. Remove the pot from the heat. Cover and let stand until the preserves are room temperature. Uncover and stir the cherries up through the syrup occasionally. Reheat just to boiling and ladle into jars that have just been scrubbed clean and rinsed out with hot water. Seal.

This amount makes about 5 half-pint jars.

Teatime Sour-Cherry Preserves

Two very simple extra steps in this recipe make these preserves extra-special: the cherry pits are used to give extra tartness and the cherries are left in the syrup overnight to allow the syrup to thicken and hold them evenly throughout the jelly.

       2 pounds black or red
         sour cherries
    4½ cups sugar
       1 cup boiling water
      ¼ cup strained fresh lemon juice

Wash, stem, and pit the cherries. Put the pits in a non-metal bowl.

Place a layer of the pitted cherries in the preserving kettle and sprinkle with sugar. Repeat layers until all cherries and sugar are used, ending with the last of the sugar.

Pour the boiling water over the cherry pits. Let stand about 15 minutes. Strain and pour the water over the cherries and sugar. Allow mixture to stand about 1 hour. Then place the kettle over high heat and bring to a full rolling boil and let boil hard for about 30 minutes or until syrup is as thick as honey. Stir frequently and skim surface often. Remove from heat and stir in the lemon juice. Cover the kettle and let stand until cool, then refrigerate covered overnight.

Next morning return the kettle to medium heat and again bring the preserves to a full boil. Boil hard for 1 minute.

Ladle into clean hot jars and seal.

Makes about 4 half-pints.

Quick and Easy
Peachy Peach Jam

10 large, hard, ripe peaches
 6 cups sugar

Peel and slice peaches about ¼ inch thick. Crack open 2 peach pits and put aside.

Combine fruit and sugar in a large non-metal bowl. Let stand overnight in the refrigerator (12 to 18 hours).

Transfer fruit and sugar to a preserving kettle, add peach pits, and stir over moderate heat until sugar has dissolved. Let simmer until peaches become clear and syrup thick, about 40 minutes. Stir frequently to prevent sticking. Remove from heat and skim surface if necessary.

Ladle, boiling hot, into clean hot jars. Seal.

Makes about 7 half-pints.

Note: To spice or not to spice? It depends. I like my breakfast jam just peachy, but for afternoon tea I like spiced jam. It depends on your taste. You can add 1 tablespoon whole cloves, ½ teaspoon whole allspice, and 1 stick of cinnamon all neatly tied up in a cheesecloth bag during cooking. Remove bag before ladling into jars.

Plum Jam

This is the most delicious jam I have ever eaten. It's a bit of trouble to stone the plums, but after that there's nothing to it. And wait until you taste plum jam on hot biscuits with a fragrant cup of coffee. You can also make an extra-special dessert by topping a scoop of vanilla ice cream with a tablespoon of plum jam, then pouring a bit of cognac over it at the last moment. Have the cognac flaming if you want a spectacular effect.

6 cups pitted plums (They can be red or purple or use wild beach plums if you can get them.)
5 cups sugar
¼ cup water
3 tablespoons grated orange rind

Combine ingredients in a preserving kettle and bring to a boil. Boil rapidly over high heat until jam tests done. Follow the refrigerator test on page 12 or use your jelly thermometer. Stir frequently to prevent scorching. Ladle into clean hot jars and seal.

Makes about 5 half-pints.

Epicurean Raspberry Jam

This recipe combines jelly-making with jam-making, so, of course, there is a little more work involved, but the results are so very good. I think you will find it worth the effort, as it's a very special jam.

1 quart red currants
4 quarts raspberries
Sugar

Pick over and wash the currants, discarding leaves and damaged berries, but do not stem them. Just put them in a colander and wash quickly under cold water.

Dump the currants with any water that clings to them into a large pot and mash them with a potato masher until the juices flow. Put the pot over medium heat and let them cook as you continue to mash for about 10 minutes.

Allow the mush to drip through a colander lined with a triple thickness of cheesecloth and set over a large bowl. It will take time to obtain all the juices, but you can mash the fruit to help it along. Unlike jelly, it doesn't matter if the juice is not crystal clear.

Put the raspberries in a large bowl—or the kitchen sink—fill with cold water. Swish them around so that the dirt and sand will sink to the bottom, then lift them out and combine them with the currant juice. Measure the mixture and to each cup of berries and juice add an equal measure of sugar. Blend and transfer to your preserving kettle.

Place the kettle over medium heat and stir gently with a long wooden spoon until the sugar has dissolved. Increase the heat and let the mixture boil hard until a small amount of it will hold its shape on a cold saucer after being placed in the freezer for a few moments. Stir often. Twenty minutes should give you a jam of just the right consistency.

Remove from heat and skim the surface carefully, then stir to distribute the fruit. Ladle into clean hot jars and seal.

Makes about 5 half-pint jars.

All-Year Raspberry Jam

To my way of thinking, no other jam can touch raspberry with its wild tart-sweet taste.

Incredibly good on hot breads for breakfast, the

perfect jam for an English trifle, and super delicious spread on a jelly roll. The trouble is raspberries are fragile, temperamental things, hard to get even when in season and usually terribly expensive. The answer is, of course, to make your raspberry jam from frozen berries any time you feel like it. It's easy and quick to do and far less expensive than commercial raspberry jam, which at its best is never anywhere near home-made. This recipe is simply the classic combination of fruit and sugar. You can use pectin to make very good raspberry jam and the yield will be greater, but I prefer to keep the intense raspberry flavor and just be "sparing" with servings.

2 10-ounce boxes frozen raspberries
2 cups sugar

Combine raspberries and sugar in a preserving kettle and bring to a boil over high heat. Boil rapidly until jam is quite thick, about 30 minutes. Stir your raspberry jam frequently; it will scorch if you're not careful. Ladle into clean hot jars and seal. What could be simpler—or better?

Makes 2 half-pint jars.

Classic Strawberry Jam

2½ quarts strawberries
6½ cups sugar
 ¼ cup lemon juice

Hull the berries. Put them in a big bowl of cold water and swish them around so that all sand and dirt filters to the bottom. Scoop them up and put them in a big non-metal bowl. Add the sugar and lemon juice and toss to distribute evenly. It's easier to use your hands for this job. Cover the bowl and let stand several hours to draw out the berry juice.

Transfer the mixture to the preserving kettle. A large one is an absolute necessity because the jam boils up quite a bit.

Place over moderate heat and stir gently with a long wooden spoon until the sugar dissolves. Increase the heat and let the mixture boil hard for 20 to 25 minutes or until moderately thickened. The jam will thicken as it stands, so don't overcook. Remove from the heat and let cool a bit, then pour the jam back into your big bowl and again let stand several hours. This plumps up the fruit and allows the jam to thicken so that the berries will be evenly distributed and not float to the top in the jar.

Ladle into clean hot jars and seal with paraffin.

Makes about 8 half-pints.

Strawberry Melba Jam

6 cups pureed strawberries
   (about 5 pints)
3 cups raspberries
6 cups sugar
3 tablespoons grated orange rind
1 tablespoon grated lemon rind
2 tablespoons lemon juice

Combine all ingredients in large kettle. Bring slowly to a boil, stirring almost constantly. Cook over moderate heat, stirring frequently until moderately thickened, 30 to 45 minutes. The jam thickens as it stands, so do not overcook. Remove from heat, ladle immediately into clean hot jars, and seal.

Makes about 7 half-pint jars.

Sun-Cooked Strawberry Jam

You'll need a blistering hot, frantically sunny day to do this, but it's fun and is about the only reason I can think of to be grateful for a blistering hot, frantically sunny day. Some people say this is the best jam ever.

2 quarts small, ripe but firm,
   unblemished strawberries
8 cups sugar

Prepare your equipment first. Put a kitchen table in the full sun, each leg set in small pan of water to keep ants or other small crawling insects from the jam. To protect the jam from flying insects, have ready a large sheet of clean window glass that you have bound in tape to protect your fingers. You will also need some means to prop the glass at a slant over the platters of jam (I use 2 clean bricks), as well as cheesecloth to tape, like a curtain, around the 3 sides left open to the air.

Wash and hull the berries. Put a layer of them into your widest deep enamel pan and cover with sugar. Repeat until all berries are used, ending with the last of the sugar. Let stand for about 1 hour to let the juice start to flow.

Place over low heat and cook, stirring gently, until the sugar has dissolved.

Pour syrupy berries about ½ inch deep into long,

shallow, glass baking pans and put them on the table in strong sun. Prop the glass over them with one edge on the table, the opposite edge raised about 4 inches high (this allows any condensation to run down the glass onto the table and not into the jam). Tape cheesecloth around the open sides.

Move the table as needed to keep it in the direct sun and turn the jam with a spatula several times during the sun cooking.

When thick as jam should be, ladle it into clean jars and seal with paraffin.

Raspberry and blackberry jam can be cooked in the same way, but they are not washed.

Tomato Jam

Cassia buds make this a different and sophisticated "main course" jam. It goes equally well with meat or chicken dishes or you can add additional spices—ground ginger, mace, turmeric, or mustard—for a jam to give to a devotee of curry.

24 large ripe tomatoes
Sugar
 2 teaspoons cassia buds tied
    securely in a cheesecloth bag

You may substitute sticks of cinnamon, but the cassia gives a more delicate flavor.

The tomatoes must be skinned because the skins separate from the pulp and become tough and stringy. The easiest way to go about this is to place a single layer of the tomatoes in a large, flat-bottomed pan, pour boiling water over them, and let them stand for a full minute. Then remove them one at a time with a long, 2-pronged kitchen fork, hold under cold running water, and with the help of a small sharp knife slip off the skins. The water should be boiling—really hot—but the tomatoes should not stay overlong in it, so it's best to work in small batches of 6 or 8, using freshly boiled water each time.

When all the tomatoes are skinned, chop them coarsely, measure, and place them in a large preserving pot. Add a cup of sugar for each cup of tomatoes and place over low, really low, heat. Mash the tomatoes with a heavy wooden spoon until the juices flow and the sugar has dissolved. Add the cheesecloth bag of cassia buds and let the mixture cook over the lowest possible heat until very thick. This will take from 2 to 2½ hours. This jam tends to stick, so it must be watched and stirred very frequently, but I do think you will find the results worth the trouble. There's nothing new about tomato jam, but this one has a particularly nice flavor and does make a very special gift.

Remove the cassia buds and ladle into freshly scrubbed, hot jars. Seal.

Makes about 6 half-pint jars.

California Green-Tomato Jam

Peppery hot and spiced with ginger. Serve with cold meats, with curry dishes, or—especially good—with broiled fish.

2 quarts small green tomatoes
2 large lemons
4½ cups sugar
Small slice green ginger root
4 canned California green chilies
½ cup chopped candied
orange peel

Wash and slice the tomatoes. Cut the lemons into the thinnest possible slices, then cut each slice into quarters. Remove and discard seeds.

Put a layer of the tomatoes in a large nonmetallic bowl, add a few pieces of lemon, and cover with some of the sugar. Repeat with successive layers, ending with the last of the sugar. Cover and refrigerate overnight.

Next day let the mixture come to room temperature, then prepare your remaining ingredients.

Flatten the slice of ginger root with the side of a heavy cleaver to break up the fibers and loosen the juices. Rinse the chilies under cold running water, remove the seeds, and pith and chop very fine.

Place all ingredients in your preserving kettle and stir over moderate heat until sugar has dissolved. Bring to a full boil, then lower heat and let bubble gently for about 1½ hours or until thick as you like it. Stir often to prevent burning.

Ladle into very clean hot jars and seal.

Makes about 4 half-pint jars.

Uncooked Jams
with Liqueur

Uncooked jams are the easiest of all to prepare, but I always found them rather insipid, like uncooked icing —oversweet and lacking in flavor—until I started adding liqueurs. Then the results were spectacular. They are heavenly over ice cream and do something special to sherbet, even the low-calorie type. Great for jelly

31

rolls and equally nice with cream cheese and crackers for an afternoon tea party.

It's best to work in small batches, so the following recipes make only 4 small jars, but it's easy to continue with a second batch right after the first.

Uncooked Strawberry-Brandy Jam

1 quart strawberries
Sugar
¼ to ½ cup good-quality brandy

Put the strawberries in a large bowl of cold water, swish them around a bit, and then lift them out. This is really the best way to wash any berries to retain all flavor. Blot them dry with paper towels. Place in a large bowl and mash thoroughly. I use an old-fashioned potato masher.

Measure the mashed fruit, then return it to the bowl and add an equal amount of sugar a little at a time, mixing well after each addition. Add the brandy and blend.

Pack into very clean jars to overflowing. Seal with paraffin and that's all there is to it. But I find that the flavor improves when I put the jars in a sunny window for a few hours each day for a week.

Makes 4 half-pint jars with a little left over to eat "tonight."

Uncooked Pineapple-Rum Jam

1 large pineapple
Sugar
¼ to ½ cup white rum

Slice, pare, and core the pineapple, then chop very fine. Measure and place in a large bowl. Add an equal amount of sugar a little at a time, blending well after each addition. Add the rum. Blend and pack to overflowing in very clean jars. Seal with paraffin.

Uncooked Raspberry-Peach Brandy Jam

1 quart raspberries
Sugar
¼ to ½ cup peach brandy or
    peach liqueur

Follow instructions for strawberry-brandy jam.

To Speak of Jellies

My grandfather used to make mayhaw jelly every summer. It was crystal-clear, a sparkling wild pink in color, and had a tart sweetness that turned baking-powder biscuits into an incredible delight.

Perhaps you've never heard of mayhaws, which grow wild in the dense pine woods of northern Louisiana. They are a form of crab apple really, small and pink and far too bitter to eat "as is," but when transformed by sugar and heat—well, there has never been such jelly. We lived near such a wood, and in summer we would roam the satiny pine-needle-covered ground in the dense shade, taking as long as possible to gather our basket of mayhaws. We always found wild ferns too, to be carefully dug and replanted in a shady spot in the garden.

But you need not wait to find wild mayhaws; crab

apples, berries of every kind, grapes, quince, mint, currants, cranberries, all can be turned into shimmering transparent jellies of ruby, pink, purple, deep dark blue, and emerald to glow like jewels on a pantry shelf and to add pure delight to every meal you serve.

For jellies are not simply an accompaniment to the breakfast roll or toast. Think of crisp roast duck with fried grits and currant jelly, broiled chicken with crab-apple jelly, crepes spread with blackberry jelly and a dollop of sour cream. What would lamb be without mint jelly? And who ever heard of turkey without cranberry?

It takes a cook with pride to make jelly. Jelly has to be strained carefully, and the cook must not be too "saving" in her ways. Try to force out the juice and the jelly will be cloudy. Patience is required, to let the fruit release its juice drop by drop, but the results are well worth the effort. Really fine homemade jelly simply cannot be bought at any price. It is a labor of love, not money.

Perfect Apple Jelly

If apple jelly doesn't sound exciting to you, it's probably because you have been getting your supply from the local supermarket. Homemade apple jelly is another thing entirely.

The best time for making apple jelly is in the early fall. Apples are at their peak just as the weather turns crisp. Actually "October's Bright Blue Weather" is apple-jelly-making time. Buy a basket of bright glowing apples at a roadside stand if possible. The next morning while the day is still cool and fresh, turn them into clear amber jelly that is truly an epicurean delight.

6 pounds tart crisp apples
 (MacIntosh variety is best.)
6 cups water
3 cups sugar

Almost all apples these days are sprayed, so wash them well under cold running water before you begin. Remove stem and blossom ends. Don't peel or core; just chop them into small pieces. Put the apples in a large pot, add the water, and bring to a full boil. Cover, lower heat and let simmer for 30 minutes or until they are very soft and mushy.

Line a large sieve or colander with a wet cloth. You can use 4 thicknesses of cheesecloth, but for really clear, sparkling jelly cotton flannel is best. I buy it by the yard; it's inexpensive and does make for beautiful results.

Place the lined colander over a large bowl and pour in the apples. Don't, for goodness' sake, mash to force the juice, or the jelly will be cloudy. Just let it filter through. The easy way is to make space in your refrigerator and leave the whole works in the cold overnight. Next morning the bowl will be filled with clear juice and you are ready to proceed.

Measure out 4 cups of the juice. I usually drink what's left over, which isn't much, but it is the most refreshing morning beverage I've ever tasted. Add the sugar to the juice in a large pot and place over high heat, stir well, and allow to come to a full boil. Let boil until it begins to jell, which should be about 15 minutes. There are several ways to test doneness, but to my way of thinking the easiest is with a cold silver spoon. Dip the spoon into the boiling jelly, lift out a spoonful, and pour it back into the pot. If the last bit forms together and falls from the spoon in a lazy drop, the jelly should be done.

Take the pot from the stove and quickly skim off foam. Ladle into clean hot jars and seal.

Makes 3 to 4 half-pint jars.

Apple-Mint Jelly

This is a lovely jelly to make on a beautiful early fall morning when apples are crisp and the sunny days have kept the mint still green in the garden. City dwellers don't despair. Mint plants are available in most seed stores and will flourish if kept well watered on a windowsill.

1 cup fresh mint leaves,
  firmly packed
1 cup boiling water
4 cups fresh apple juice (See
  preceding recipe for basic
  apple jelly.)
4 cups sugar
Green food coloring

Place the mint leaves in a small bowl and cover with boiling water. Let stand for at least 2 hours. Drain into preserving kettle and discard mint leaves. Add apple juice and sugar, stir well, and bring to a boil over high heat. Let boil until jelly tests for doneness. Remove from heat, skim, ladle into clean hot jars, and seal.

Makes 3 to 4 half-pint jars.

Easy Spiced-Apple Jelly

2¾ cups bottled unsweetened
    apple juice
 2 teaspoons allspice
 ¼ cup white wine vinegar
 4 cups sugar
Red food coloring
Yellow food coloring
 ½ bottle (3 ounces) liquid pectin

This is an excellent jelly to serve with meats or fowl and is nice too as an extra accompaniment for curry dishes.

Combine apple juice and allspice in a saucepan and bring to a full boil. Then lower heat and let simmer very gently for about 10 minutes. Strain through a sieve lined with a triple thickness of cheesecloth. You can put the sieve right over the preserving kettle and save washing an extra bowl. Add vinegar and sugar and again bring to a full rolling boil. Remove from heat. Put 1 drop of red and 1 of yellow food coloring on a silver spoon and stir this into the jelly. This will give you a deep amber hue that somehow suggests the spicy taste. Stir in the pectin and again bring to a full rolling boil and boil hard for 1 minute, stirring constantly. Remove from heat. To ensure a clear jelly, skim surface carefully of all foam. Use a silver spoon and take care not to stir the foam down into the jelly. Ladle into clean hot jars and seal.

Makes about 2 half-pint jars.

Apple-Cranberry Jelly

I think you will like this combined fruit jelly. It is more delicate than all cranberry but heartier than plain apple. It's a particularly delicious jelly to serve with roast chicken. Great too with chicken hash—split baking-powder biscuits while hot, spread with jelly, and cover with hash for a meal to remember.

2 quarts tart crisp apples
1 quart cranberries
Water
Sugar

Cut up the apples, discarding stems and blossom
ends. Put them in your preserving kettle and add the
cranberries. Pour in just enough water to barely cover
the fruit. Bring to a boil over high heat then reduce
heat to low. Cover the kettle and let simmer for about
30 minutes, or until apples are very soft and the cranberries pop open. Drain through a sieve lined with a
wet flannel cloth that has been placed over a large
bowl.

Don't mash the fruit if you want a clear jelly.

Measure juice, then measure out an equal amount of
sugar, but don't combine them yet.

Put the juice in the preserving kettle and bring it to
a full boil. Lower heat and let simmer for 5 minutes.
Add the sugar and let boil to jelling point. Stir and
skim often. When jelly sheets from the spoon, remove
the kettle from the heat and skim off the last bit of
foam. Ladle into clean hot jars and seal.

Makes about 6 half-pint jars.

Classic Cranberry Jelly

Cranberry jelly is an old favorite that's so easy to
make, so never-fail good that it shouldn't be left out
of any book about fine preserving. Yet the classic
recipe of sugar and cranberries can't be improved,
shouldn't be changed.

4 cups cranberries
2 cups water
2 cups sugar

Wash the cranberries and discard any damaged fruit.

Put them in a saucepan with the water and let boil until they are soft and the skins pop open. Strain, discarding seeds and skin.

Combine juice and sugar in your preserving kettle and stir over medium heat until sugar has dissolved. Then increase heat and let boil hard for 8 to 10 minutes or until a drop or so will turn to firm jelly when dropped on a cold saucer. It doesn't take long— no more than 10 minutes—so watch and test often.

Makes about 4 half-pint jars.

Red Currant Jelly

I don't think anyone ever tires of currant jelly. It can be used in so many ways—at breakfast, lunch, and dinner, as a spread on breakfast toast or an accompaniment to roast beef, in a tart sauce for chicken or game birds, as a sweet sauce for dessert, and as a filling for jelly roll or a glaze for fruit tarts.

2 quarts red currants
2½ cups sugar

Pick over and discard any damaged berries but do not stem them. Put them in a colander and wash quickly under cold running water, gently lifting up and turning the berries so that the water gets to all of them. Dump them still wet into the preserving kettle and mash with a wooden potato masher or a heavy glass tumbler until the juices flow. You will have a mush of berries and juice. Cook over medium heat for 10 minutes. Then let the juices drip through a sieve that you have lined with several thicknesses of cheesecloth and set over a large bowl. This will take several hours or may be left overnight.

Measure the juice and measure out an equal amount of sugar. Put the sugar in the preserving kettle and place the kettle on an asbestos pad over very low heat. Let heat without melting for about 10 minutes. Stir several times.

Heat the currant juice in a saucepan to almost boiling. Then pour it over the sugar. Boil hard, skimming and stirring constantly, until the liquid will sheet from the spoon. It takes only 5 to 6 minutes, so watch and test almost from the start. Don't overcook. Ladle into clean hot jars and seal.

Makes about 5 half-pint jars.

Epicurean Concord Grape Jelly

This is a superlative jelly. No water is added to dilute the flavor, and quick cooking retains the true taste of the fresh fruit. It's very easy to make, but you must take time to prepare the juice, or rather let the juice leisurely prepare itself.

5 pounds barely ripe Concord
  grapes with a few red underripe
4 cups sugar

Select about one-fourth underripe and three-fourths fully ripe grapes.

Wash them quickly under cold running water and

remove stems. Place them in your preserving kettle and crush with a potato masher to start the juices flowing. Cook without boiling over medium heat until soft. This will take only about 10 minutes, and you can help by mashing the fruit a bit as it cooks.

Pour the contents of the kettle into a sieve lined with a clean, wet flannel cloth and set over a large bowl. Let the juices flow through. This will take several hours, but don't try to hurry the job by mashing the fruit or your jelly will be cloudy.

The next step is one you can eliminate if you plan

on serving this jelly within a few weeks. Grape jelly has a tendency to crystallize on standing. To prevent this, let the juices stand undisturbed in your refrigerator overnight or for several hours, then strain it through several thicknesses of cheesecloth. This will eliminate any crystals that may have formed. There are usually quite a few, and although they do no harm in your jelly jars, they prevent a crystal-clear look.

When you are ready to make your jelly, measure the juice. You should have more than 5 cups. Set 1 cup aside. Put the remaining 4 cups in your preserving kettle and bring to a full rolling boil. Remove from heat and immediately dump in the sugar. Return the kettle to a second burner—the first one used will be too hot—and stir over low heat until the sugar has dissolved. This will take only a few minutes. If the grapes contained the right amount of sugar and acid, the jelly will be ready. Test, of course. If the jelly sheets from the spoon, it's ready for the jars. If not, add the remaining cup of juice and continue to cook until the jelling point has been reached. Ladle into clean hot jars and seal.

Makes 3 to 4 half-pint jars.

Honest Lemon Jelly

3 large lemons
6 cups cold water
4 cups sugar

Cut lemons into very thin slices; they should measure 2 heaping cups. Place in a glass bowl or enamel pan. Add water, cover, and let stand for about 18 hours. Transfer to a stainless steel or enamel saucepan. Bring to a boil, reduce heat, and simmer, covered, for 40 minutes. Over a large bowl, place a colander or strainer lined with several layers of cheesecloth and pour cooked lemon slices and water into it. Let the juice drain through undisturbed; do not press lemon slices down to speed up the process. When lemons stop dripping, measure juice. If the juice measures more than 4 cups, boil rapidly until reduced to 4 cups.

Combine prepared juice and sugar in a large kettle. Stir over moderate heat until sugar dissolves. Boil rapidly over moderately high heat, stirring frequently. When liquid sheets from spoon, remove from heat. For a yellow color, stir in a few drops yellow food coloring. Quickly skim off foam and ladle into hot jelly glasses or jelly jars. Fill to within ¼ inch of top. Seal.

Makes 4 half-pint glasses or jars.

Easy Madeira Jelly

Good with meat, any meat.

3½ cups sugar
 ½ cup water
 ¾ cup Madeira wine
 ½ bottle (3 ounces) liquid pectin
 2 6-ounce cans frozen
   unsweetened grape juice
   concentrate, thawed

Place sugar, water, and wine in a large, heavy saucepan and stir over low heat until sugar dissolves. Increase heat and bring to a full rolling boil. I do mean a rolling boil that can't be stirred down. Boil for a full minute then remove from heat and immediately stir in the pectin. Add the completely thawed grape juice concentrate and stir until well blended. Skim off any foam, then ladle immediately into clean hot jars. Seal with paraffin.

Makes 4 or 5 half-pint jars.

Hot Pepper Jelly

```
 4  large green peppers
12  dried hot red peppers
 7  cups sugar
1½  cups high-quality white vinegar
 2  or 3 drops green food coloring
 2  bottles (12 ounces)
    liquid pectin
```

Cut green peppers into strips, discarding seeds and white fibers, and chop very fine. Place in preserving kettle. Crumble and add the dried red peppers. Add sugar and vinegar. Place over medium heat and bring to a full boil. Lower heat and let simmer for 10 minutes. Strain through a colander lined with 4 thicknesses of cheesecloth into a second large kettle. The easy way is to let the mixture cool slightly, then use a ladle or cup to pour the mixture through a little at a time.

When the liquid has been strained, add the food coloring. It's advisable to drop the coloring onto a spoon and then stir it into the jelly because it's easy to add more than you need. Aim for the clear, cool color of green peppers.

Stir in pectin. Return the mixture to the heat and again bring to a boil. Boil 1 minute.

Have your jars ready—very clean and dry but still

45

warm from rinsing with hot water—and ladle the jelly into them immediately, as this jelly jells very fast. Seal while hot.

Makes about 7 half-pint jars.

Parsley Jelly

2 large bunches parsley
3 quarts water
5 cups sugar
2 teaspoons grated lemon rind
1½ cup lime juice
½ bottle (3 ounces)
    liquid fruit pectin
Green food coloring

Wash parsley well and place in kettle with water. Bring to a boil, reduce heat, and simmer, covered, for 20 minutes. Strain; discard parsley. Measure the juice, return it to the kettle and boil rapidly until reduced to 3 cups.

Combine 3 cups parsley juice, sugar, lemon rind, and lime juice in preserving kettle. Stir over moderate heat until sugar dissolves and mixture comes to a boil. Stir in liquid pectin all at once and, continuing to stir, bring to a full rolling boil and boil hard for 1 minute. Remove from heat. For a pale green color, stir in a few drops green food coloring. Quickly skim off foam and ladle into hot jars. Fill jars to within ¼ inch of top. Seal.

Makes 5 half-pint jars.

Easy Pineapple-Lime Jelly

3½ cups sugar
1¼ cups water
½ bottle (3 ounces) liquid pectin
1 can (6 ounces) frozen
  pineapple juice concentrate,
  thawed
3 tablespoons lime juice

Combine the sugar and water in a large, heavy saucepan and stir over medium heat until sugar dissolves.
Then bring to a full rolling boil and boil 1 minute,
stirring constantly.

Remove from heat and immediately stir in liquid
pectin. Add pineapple juice and mix well. Skim off the
foam with a metal spoon. Ladle into clean hot jars
and seal. Makes about 5 half-pint jars of jelly.

Easy Sauterne Jelly

Fine with roast chicken.

1 cup freshly squeezed,
  strained grapefruit juice
1 cup dry California sauterne
3½ cups sugar
½ bottle (3 ounces) liquid pectin

Place grapefruit juice, sauterne, and sugar in a large
saucepan and stir over low heat until sugar dissolves
and mixture begins to boil. This takes only about 5
minutes, but you must stir the entire time.

Remove from heat and immediately stir in the

pectin. Skim off the foam with a metal spoon and ladle right away into clean hot jars and seal.

You should get 5 full half-pint jars with maybe a little left over.

Easy Red-Hot Tomato Jelly

This is a hot and lively jelly to serve with meat. I particularly like it with old-fashioned corned beef and cabbage, but it's also good on hot breads—like cornbread served with southern-style fried fish.

1 3/4 cup nonalcoholic
     bloody mary mix
1/2 cup strained lemon juice
  2 teaspoons Tabasco sauce
  4 cups sugar
1/2 bottle (3 ounces) liquid pectin

Combine all ingredients except pectin in a large, heavy saucepan. Stir over high heat until mixture comes to a full rolling boil. Remove from heat and stir in pectin. Then again bring to a full rolling boil and boil for 1 minute over high heat. Remove from heat and stir and skim for about 3 minutes. Ladle into clean hot jars and seal.

Makes from 5 to 6 half-pint jars.

To Speak of Marmalade

As Lord Emsworth, the squire of Blandings Castle in P. G. Wodehouse's famous chronicle of Bertie Wooster and Jeeves, often said, "There's nothing like roly poly pudding if there's lots of marmalade." No doubt, and there's nothing like a hot buttered scone spread with the tart sweetness of real marmalade.

Marmalade has a fascination for me. It conjures up all sorts of memories—of a country house in the Cotswolds with a tea table set in front of a roaring fire, of London's rose brick houses in Curzon Street, their black chimney pots etched against a misty gray sky. In particular I remember breakfast at Brown's Hotel—a proper English breakfast of eggs, kippers, tea, scones, and of course marmalade. What marmalade it was too, made of bitter Seville oranges cooked to amber perfection. I begged the recipe from the stout, red-faced cook, and it's here for you to try.

There are all sorts of marmalades to be sure, even cherry marmalade, first made for Queen Henrietta Maria, the consort of Charles the First, by someone known as "Madam Mancy." Whoever the good lady was, her directions are somewhat vague, so I've included my own here, a bit more dependable but still retaining the royal touch.

But to my way of thinking, marmalade is best made from oranges, lemons, and limes. I love the fragrance of their citrus sweetness and the delicacy and freshness of their orange, yellow, and green coloring. To cheer yourself up on a raw January day, order a supply of these beautiful fruits along with a bag of sugar and transform your mood and your house with the color

49

and fragrance of real homemade marmalade. And what an addition to your gift shelf—(if this is one of your friends' fancies).

Brown's Hotel Whisky Marmalade

Bitter Seville oranges and scotch whisky are the ingredients used in making classic British marmalade, but since these oranges are hard to come by in this country, I have found that large California oranges plus lemons are an acceptable substitute. However, the whisky is indispensable. A good marmalade can be made without it, but it is this ingredient as much as the type of oranges that makes this marmalade a classic.

6 large California oranges
2 medium lemons
1 quart water
1 pint scotch whisky (You can
  use more whisky and less water
  if you feel like being extravagant,
  but a pint will give the necessary
  flavor.)
Sugar

Using your sharpest small knife, peel the thin colored skin from the oranges and the lemons. Then cut the peel into very narrow strips about 1 inch long. Place peeled fruit in plastic bags and refrigerate. Place peel in a large non-metal bowl. Add the water and whisky. Cover and set aside in a cool place—not the refrigerator, however—for 18 to 24 hours.

When you are ready to proceed, first use your kitchen shears to cut the oranges and lemons into large

50

pieces. Do this over a large bowl to retain all the juices. Remove all the seeds but don't discard them; tie them in a small cheesecloth bag and set aside. Next put the chopped fruit through a food chopper or use a sharp knife to chop it as finely as possible.

Measure fruit, juice, and peel, then measure and set aside an equal quantity of sugar.

Put the peel, the whisky and water, the pulp, and the juice in the preserving kettle and place over low heat. Let boil until the peel is very soft, about 2 hours. Add the sugar and stir over moderate heat until sugar dissolves. Add the bag of seeds to the mixture, bring to a gentle boil, and boil to the jelling point. Stir occasionally at first, then very often as mixture begins to thicken.

Remove the bag of seeds and ladle the marmalade into freshly scrubbed jars. Seal.

Makes 6 to 7 half-pint jars.

Three-Day Florida Grapefruit Marmalade

This is an easy recipe that takes time to prepare but very little actual work, and the results are excellent— a sweet marmalade of just the right consistency.

1 large grapefruit
2 large thick-skinned oranges
1 large lemon
3 quarts water
Sugar

Don't peel. Just cut all the fruits into thin slivers, discarding seeds. You will need a sharp knife to do this job properly. The slivers should be as nearly the same size as possible—matchstick thin, from ½ to 1 inch in length. Put all in a large, deep, non-metal bowl and cover with the water. Cover the bowl with foil and put it in the refrigerator to soak the fruit for 24 hours. Transfer to preserving kettle and bring to a boil over medium heat. Then let boil for 15 minutes. Return mixture to bowl and again let soak for 24 hours.

Drain and measure fruit. Add 1 cup of sugar for each cup of fruit and—here we go again—let stand 24 hours. After this—yes, finally—it's ready to cook.

Place over moderate heat and bring to a full boil. Let boil gently until the syrup drops heavily from a spoon. Time varies from 30 to 45 minutes and sometimes even a little longer—it depends on the fruit—but don't overcook or the syrup will become sugary.

If this sounds tricky, believe me it's not. Just stir often and keep an eye on the kettle and you'll soon have 4 half-pint jars of marmalade of which you can be justly proud.

Lemon-Lime Marmalade

4 large lemons
4 large limes
1½ quarts water
Sugar, about 5½ cups

The quality of the fruit is doubly important here. It should be top-notch—large, juicy, and fragrant with perfect, unblemished skins.

With a small sharp knife cut the thin outer peel— the yellow and green part—from the fruit. Cut the peel with your kitchen shears into thin strips about ½ inch long.

Working over a large bowl and again with your shears, cut the peeled fruit into small pieces, discarding seeds and cores.

Put the peel and fruit and all the juices that you have collected in the bowl into the preserving kettle. Add the water and bring to a full boil. Remove from heat, cool, then cover and refrigerate the entire works overnight.

Next day bring again to a full boil and let boil until the peel is quite tender. This will take about 45 minutes.

Cool, then refrigerate once more overnight.

Now measure the fruit and juice and return it to the kettle and add an equal amount of sugar. Stir over moderate heat until the sugar dissolves, then boil hard to jelling point. Liquid should sheet from a cold metal spoon.

Remove from heat and allow to cool to room temperature. Stir the marmalade well to distribute the peel evenly and ladle into clean hot jars. Seal with paraffin.

Makes 5 or 6 half-pint jars.

Peach-Orange Marmalade

10 large ripe peaches
 2 medium oranges
 1 large lemon
 5 cups sugar

Peel and chop peaches. Peel the oranges and cut the peel into thin slivers. Chop the orange pulp. Cut the lemon into paper-thin slices and quarter each slice.

Combine all ingredients in your preserving kettle and stir over medium heat until sugar dissolves. Increase heat to high and let boil hard for about 20 minutes or until liquid sheets from a cold metal spoon. Stir frequently to prevent sticking.

Ladle into clean hot jars and seal.

Makes about 8 half-pint jars.

Milenda's Marmalade

This is a quick and easy recipe that's thrifty too. The combined fruits add up to a not-too-sweet but mellow flavor. Everyone at our house pronounces it extra good.

1 small grapefruit
5 large oranges
2 large lemons
2 cups water
7 cups sugar
1 bottle (6 ounces) liquid pectin

Cut the outer peel from the grapefruit, oranges, and lemons, removing only a small part of the white. Use your kitchen shears to cut the peel into thin slivers. Put them in your preserving kettle, add the water, and bring to a boil. Lower heat, cover the kettle, and let simmer for 30 minutes. Set the kettle aside, away from the heat. Cut the remaining peel from the fruit and separate the fruit into sections. Remove seeds and cut each section into small pieces. Do this over a large bowl to catch all the juices.

Add the cut fruit to the rind and water in the preserving kettle. Add the sugar. Stir over moderate heat until sugar dissolves and mixture comes to a boil. Stir in pectin and continue to stir, bringing to a full rolling boil. Then let boil hard for a full minute.

Remove from heat and quickly skim off any foam. Ladle into clean hot jars and seal. Invert for a few seconds, then let jars cool to room temperature. This will take from 4 to 5 hours. Turn jars, first inverted, then upright, every hour or until the rind and sections no longer float to the top.

Makes 8 half-pint jars.

To Speak of Conserves

Conserves are the "haute couture" of the preserving world. They are marvelous mixes of plums, peaches, pears, apples, each laced with plump dark raisins, amber ginger, nuts, bits of crystallized orange and lemon peel. Here are the dazzlers, the beaded glittery creations, not the simple unadorned basics. There is always a touch of the exotic in a conserve, a sense of adventure and a whiff of romance—perhaps from the lingering remembrance that conserves originated in Persia, where apricots, pomegranates, honey, and rose petals were "conserved" in turquoise-encrusted jars.

An adventurous and sophisticated cook is needed for the making of conserves; they are not for the timid, and an adventurous hand is needed for the serving. Try orange and pear conserve with slices of cold roast meat or chicken, accompanied by hot corn fritters and perhaps a glass of champagne. Transform lowly hamburgers by broiling, then spreading with red pepper conserve, and broiling one second more. Add crisp fried onion rings, slices of cold tomatoes, and a cold glass of beer. For a spectacular dessert add peach conserve to a combination of vanilla ice cream and orange sherbet, plus a tablespoon of cognac or Grand Marnier for each serving.

When you become a conserve addict, as I am, you'll think of your own combinations of fruits and seasonings. Meanwhile, here are my favorites to start you on your way.

Winter Apple Conserve

    8 crisp tart apples
    1 cup raisins
    3 cups sugar
    ½ cup chopped candied ginger
    ¼ cup chopped candied orange peel
    ¾ cup orange juice
    1 teaspoon cinnamon
    1 teaspoon ginger
    ½ teaspoon nutmeg
    ½ teaspoon salt
    ½ cup coarsely chopped walnuts

Wash the apples and chop them into very small cubes.

Chop the raisins and add them to the apples in the preserving kettle. Add remaining ingredients except walnuts. Start with very moderate heat, and when the sugar has dissolved, let the mixture boil gently for about 30 minutes. Stir often. Add walnuts during last 5 minutes of cooking.

Ladle into clean hot jars. Seal.

This makes a great pre-Christmas gift since, with the addition of a little butter and a bit of brandy, it's a glorious substitute for mincemeat in holiday puddings and pies.

Makes about 4 half-pint jars.

A Cranberry-Apple Conserve for Thanksgiving

4 large crisp apples
1 large orange
1 cup water
3 cups cranberries
4 cups sugar
1 cup coarsely chopped walnuts

Peel, core, and chop the apples, reserving about half of the peelings.

Cut the orange into the thinnest possible slices and remove seeds. Place the orange slices and the reserved apple peelings in a small saucepan with the water and let simmer over moderate heat until the skin of the orange slices is quite tender. Strain, reserving the liquid. Discard the apple peelings. Cut each orange slice into 8 small sections.

Put the apples and cranberries through a food chopper, then combine in the preserving kettle with the sugar, the orange sections, and the reserved orange–apple peeling liquid. Cook the whole works over low heat until thick, about 40 minutes. Stir frequently so that the mixture won't burn or stick, and add the walnuts during the last 5 minutes of cooking.

Ladle into clean hot jars. Seal.

Makes 4 or 5 half-pint jars. Cranberry red and delicious!

Charleston's Benne-Seed Fig Conserve

Locally grown sesame seeds are called benne seeds in Charleston, where you can buy benne wafers (crisp sesame-seed cookies), benne bars (like peanut candy), and benne seeds by the bag, to be toasted and used like—well, like sesame seeds in fig jam.

This is another preserve that can be served with the main course at dinner as well as in the usual way for breakfast.

4 tablespoons sesame seeds
2 pounds firm but ripe figs
4 cups sugar
2 cups water
4 thin slices of lemon

Preheat oven to 350°F.

Spread the sesame seeds out on a cookie sheet and bake, stirring occasionally, until lightly toasted, about 20 minutes.

Combine the sugar, water, and lemon slices in the preserving kettle. Bring to a boil, then lower heat and let simmer for about 20 minutes.

Peel the figs and add them to the simmering syrup. Cook about 30 minutes or until clear. Ladle figs into 4 hot clean half-pint jars. Add 1 lemon slice and 1 tablespoon sesame seeds to each jar.

Boil syrup for an additional 10 minutes or until thick as honey. Pour over fruit to ¼ inch of top of jars. Seal.

Makes 4 half-pint jars.

Grape Conserve

8 generous cups stemmed
   Concord Grapes
   (about 4 pounds)
Water
1 large orange
6 cups sugar
1 cup seedless raisins
¼ teaspoon allspice
½ teaspoon salt
1 cup chopped walnuts

Wash the grapes under cold running water and drain. Pinch out the inside pulp and reserve. Put the skins in the preserving kettle and add only enough water to barely cover (about ½ cup). Cook for 15 minutes. Remove the kettle from the heat. Pour off any remaining cooking water and set aside.

Put the pulp in a large, heavy saucepan and cook over moderate heat until soft, about 10 minutes. Strain through a fine sieve to remove seeds.

Add the strained pulp and all remaining ingredients except walnuts to the grape skins in the preserving kettle. Cook, stirring often, over low heat until sugar dissolves. Increase heat to high and cook, stirring constantly, for 10 minutes. Stir in the walnuts and cook, not forgetting to stir, a final 5 minutes. Ladle into hot clean jars and seal.

Makes about 7 half-pint jars.

Mr. Muller's Red Pepper Conserve

I discovered pepper jellies, jams, and conserves when I moved to Charleston. Seems like everyone has a favorite recipe, all very good. This one is sweet but spicy hot and delicious. It is excellent with any kind of meat, as well as with cream cheese and crackers.

1 dozen dried red peppers
3 green bell peppers
2 tablespoons salt
3 cups sugar
2 cups white vinegar
½ pound red cinnamon candy
1 bottle (6 ounces) liquid pectin

Crumble red pepper. Remove seeds and all "white" from the green peppers and chop fine. Place red and green peppers in a non-metal bowl. Sprinkle with salt and let stand for 3 to 4 hours. Place in a colander and rinse under cold water. Transfer to a large pot. Add sugar and vinegar and bring to a boil. Stir in cinnamon candy. Lower heat and let simmer until mixture thickens, stirring often, lifting mixture from bottom of the pot. Add pectin and continue to cook for a final minute. Ladle into clean hot jars and seal.

Makes 4 to 5 half-pint jars.

Rhubarb-Fig Conserve

½ pound dried figs
1 cup seedless raisins
1 small lemon
1 large orange
2 pounds rhubarb
2 pounds sugar
½ cup broken walnuts

Use your kitchen shears to cut the figs into small pieces. Wet the shears with cold water occasionally. Work over a non-metal bowl and you'll be finished in short order. Dump the raisins into the same bowl. Mix them around with the fig pieces, then add enough water to cover. Let stand overnight.

With a sharp knife cut the lemon and orange into the thinnest possible slices and cut each slice into four wedges.

Wash and chop the rhubarb. Put the lemon and orange wedges, the chopped rhubarb, and the sugar in a second bowl and let this also stand overnight. If you live in the South, as I do, and must contend with ants that can positively smell sugar from a mile away, you will need to store both bowls in the refrigerator. Ants—at least the ones near my house—like the sugar in raisins too.

Next day transfer the rhubarb mixture to your preserving kettle. Drain and add the figs and raisins.

Place the kettle over moderate heat and bring to a boil. Lower heat and let simmer, stirring often, until mixture will hold its shape when a spoonful is dropped on a cold saucer. Add the walnuts, stirring them down into the conserve, and cook a final 5 minutes. Ladle into clean hot jars and seal.

Makes about 8 half-pint jars.

Strawberry-Pineapple Conserve with Almonds

1½ quarts strawberries
1 1-pound can crushed pineapple
4 cups sugar
¼ cup strained fresh
   lemon juice
1 cup blanched slivered almonds

Hull and wash the strawberries. Drain the crushed pineapple and save the juice for another use—perhaps pineapple lemonade.

Put the berries, pineapple, sugar, and lemon juice in a large, deep preserving kettle. Crush the berries a bit in the sugar and then let everything stand for about 30 minutes at room temperature. This is to let the acid of the lemon juice and the berries liquefy the sugar. Place over high heat and stir until sugar dissolves completely, then let boil hard for 15 minutes, stirring very frequently. Add the slivered almonds during the last 5 minutes of cooking. Don't forget to skim as the mixture cooks and a final time before ladling into clean hot jars.

Makes about 6 half-pint jars.

Strawberry-Rhubarb Conserve

Here's a conserve of deep, rich red color, interesting texture, and delectable taste. The trick here is to find all three fresh fruits at your market. As with all conserves, the rest is easy, even the preparation.

2 quarts strawberries
1 pint red currants
1 pound rhubarb
1 1-pound can pineapple chunks, drained
1 lemon
8½ cups sugar

Preheat oven to 375°F.

Wash and hull the strawberries. Look over and wash the currants. Slice the lemon paper thin, quarter the slices, and discard the seeds.

Put all ingredients in a large roasting pan and bake for 1 hour.

Transfer the mixture to your preserving kettle and cook, stirring frequently, over fairly high heat until the juices will sheet from a cold metal spoon. This won't take long, so it's best to stay with it.

Ladle into clean hot jars and seal.

Makes about a dozen half-pint jars.

Yellow-Tomato Conserve

2 quarts small yellow tomatoes
3 cups sugar
1 teaspoon salt
1 cup seedless raisins
1 lemon, thinly sliced
4 tablespoons thinly sliced candied
    ginger (or use 4 tablespoons
    ginger root)

Wash and dry tomatoes. Cut a thin slice from blossom end and press out seeds. Combine tomatoes with sugar and salt and simmer until sugar is dissolved. Add raisins. Bring slowly to a boil, stirring constantly. Boil gently for about 40 minutes or until syrup thickens. Add lemon slices and ginger. Continue boiling about 10 minutes. Remove from heat and ladle immediately into clean hot jars. Seal.

Makes about 4 half-pint jars.

Parisian Conserve

2 medium oranges

1 large ripe pineapple

2 pounds tart cooking apples
(or enough to make 4 cups
chopped, peeled, and cored
apples)

2 cups water

1 cup white raisins

6 cups sugar

1 can (3½ ounces)
flaked coconut

Remove the outer peel from the oranges. (An old-fashioned little gadget called a vegetable peeler does this job nicely, as you want none of the white part of the rind.) Now use your kitchen shears to cut the peel into thin slivers.

Cut off the remaining peel from the oranges and break into sections. Cut the sections (over a large bowl to catch all the juices) into small pieces. As you come across the seeds, remove and discard them.

Peel the pineapple, cut away any brown spots, and cut the fruit into small cubes.

Peel, core, and chop the apples.

Combine orange peel and sections, pineapple cubes, and diced apples in the preserving kettle. Add the water and bring slowly to a boil. Reduce heat, cover the kettle, and let simmer for about 15 minutes. Add the raisins and sugar and stir until sugar dissolves. Add the coconut and increase the heat to very high. Let boil hard for 20 to 30 minutes, stirring almost constantly, until the mixture reaches the jelling stage. Ladle into clean hot jars and seal.

Makes 8 half-pint jars.

Note: Here's the easiest way I have found to prepare the pineapple. Cut off top and stem ends, place it on your cutting board, and cut off the peel in lengthwise strips. Remove brown part with the point of a small sharp knife. Quarter, cut away the core, then cut the fruit into cubes.

Low-Calorie Jellies
Mint Jelly

Think of roast leg of lamb. Dieter's delight. Lean and low in calories, but it deserves mint jelly. This version is excellent if I do say so, and weight watchers will love you for serving it.

1 cup boiling water
1 cup chopped fresh mint, firmly packed
2 tablespoons unflavored gelatin
1½ cups bottled unsweetened apple juice
1 tablespoon lemon juice
3 tablespoons Sugar Twin sugar substitute
Green food coloring

Pour the boiling water over the mint leaves in a small bowl and let stand for 2 hours. Strain, pressing the juice from the leaves.

Pour ½ cup of this mint water into a small bowl and sprinkle the gelatin over it to soften.

Bring the apple juice to a full boil. Remove from heat and add the softened gelatin. Stir until dissolved. Add the lemon juice and stir in the sugar substitute. Put 2 or 3 drops of food coloring on a teaspoon and stir into the mixture. Don't overdo, but aim for a pale mint color. Return to heat and again bring to a full boil, stirring constantly. Let boil only a few seconds. Pour into 2 just washed and still hot half-pint jars, and seal. Store in refrigerator.

Basil Jelly

Prepare as for mint jelly but substitute ½ cup fresh chopped basil (or 6 tablespoons dried basil) for the chopped mint. Instead of green use 2 drops yellow and 2 drops red food coloring.

Marjoram Jelly

Prepare as for mint jelly but substitute ¼ cup fresh marjoram (or 4 tablespoons dried) for the chopped mint. Use a light-handed blend of yellow and red food coloring.

Rosemary Jelly

Prepare as for mint jelly but substitute ¼ cup fresh (or 2 tablespoons dried) rosemary for chopped mint. Use red instead of green food coloring.

Low-Calorie Grape-Wine Jelly

This is a lovely low-calorie jelly to serve, perhaps as a dessert with crackers and cheese. Try it with Camembert and those crisp little water biscuits that come packed in a tin. It's also great as an accompaniment to roast turkey or broiled chicken.

2 tablespoons unflavored gelatin
½ cup Tokay wine
1½ cups bottled unsweetened grape juice
2 tablespoons Sugar Twin sugar substitute

This is another quickie, so prepare your jars before you begin.

Sprinkle the gelatin over the wine in a small bowl to soften.

In a large saucepan bring the grape juice to a full boil.

Remove from heat and stir in the softened gelatin, stirring until dissolved. Stir in the sugar substitute.

Bring again to a full rolling boil.

Fill jars to ¼ inch of top. Place lids on jars and screw bands tight. Invert for 1 minute, then stand jars upright to cool.

Store in refrigerator.

Makes 2 half-pint jars.

Low-Calorie Blueberry Jam

2 tablespoons lemon juice
6 tablespoons water
1 envelope unflavored gelatin
1 pint fresh blueberries
½ cup water
¾ cup Sugar Twin
   sugar substitute
½ bottle (3 ounces) liquid pectin

Combine lemon juice and the 6 tablespoons of water in a small bowl. Sprinkle gelatin over surface to soften.

Wash berries under cold water. Drain. Remove and discard any damaged fruit. Crush thoroughly with a potato masher. Measure 1½ cups crushed berries. Combine with the ½ cup water in a deep, heavy saucepan. Bring to a full boil. Remove from heat. Stir in softened gelatin and sugar substitute. Return pan again to heat, bring mixture to a full rolling boil, and boil hard for 1 minute, stirring constantly. Remove from heat once more and stir in pectin. Stir for about 5 minutes, skimming off foam as necessary. Ladle into well-scrubbed and rinsed jars. Cool and cover with plastic wrap or foil. Store in refrigerator. Will keep 2 to 3 weeks.

Makes 2 to 3 half-pint jars.

Low-Calorie Strawberry Preserves

2 pints strawberries
2 envelopes (2 tablespoons)
   unflavored gelatin
3 tablespoons cold water
⅓ cup sugar

Wash and hull strawberries, blot dry with paper toweling.

Coarse-chop about ¼ of the berries. Crush remaining berries to a pulp.

Combine gelatin and water in a saucepan. Heat, stirring constantly, until gelatin is dissolved. Add sliced and crushed berries to gelatin mixture. Stir in sugar. Bring to a boil over medium heat, stirring constantly. Lower heat and let simmer for about 2 minutes. Pour into jars. Cover and store in refrigerator.

Makes about 3 half-pint jars.

Low-Calorie Apple Jelly

1 envelope unflavored gelatin
2 cups unsweetened apple juice
1 tablespoon lemon juice
½ cup sugar
½ bottle liquid pectin
1 drop red food coloring

Sprinkle gelatin over apple juice in a large saucepan. Let soften for 1 minute. Heat to boiling, stirring constantly, until gelatin is dissolved. Add lemon juice, sugar, and liquid pectin. Bring to a full boil and let boil for 1 minute, stirring constantly.

Remove from heat and quickly skim off foam. Stir in red food coloring. Pour into jars. Cover and store in refrigerator.

Makes 2 half-pint jars.

To Speak of Chutney

To speak of chutney is to speak of India, of emeralds and rubies, of tea and rice, of cloves, pepper, cardamom, and ginger—and, of course, to speak of curry. Curries that required not one "boy" to serve the accompaniments but seven or even nine, and pity the hostess who dared offer less.

And what is curry without chutney? One might as well serve it without rice, and of course, one *must* serve curry at least several times a year. If you are not a curry addict, then you have not eaten a proper one. My own introduction to this seductive dish came at the Oberoi Grand Hotel in Calcutta's Chowringhee Road. It was no less than a nine-boy curry served from polished brass and lacquer bowls and simply incredibly good.

Naturally the Oberoi's chutney was equally superb, and it is here for you to add to your chutney repertoire. But chutney is not just an accompaniment to curry, glorious though the combination may be. Chutney goes with many things, like hard-cooked eggs, cold meats of every variety, or topping cream cheese spread on melba toast at teatime, glazing a meat loaf, or adding glamour to a roast of pork (spread the roast with chutney about 5 minutes before you take it from the oven). The point is to look upon chutney as the superb condiment it is and be grateful to the British raj who invented it.

All sorts of fruit can be used for curry besides the classic mangoes—tomatoes, apples, melon, even peaches and pears—but all benefit by a generous hand with the spices and peppers. After all, if one wants a mild-mannered jam there are many delicious ones to make, but chutney must have vigor and character. It is not the ingénue of the performance but the dashing hero who saves the day by turning the dullest dish into a smashing success.

Apple-Raisin Chutney

I've found this a great accompaniment to baked ham. It's tart but sweet and can be served in place of either a relish or a jam. For an exotic hamburger, bring the chutney to room temperature, spread it on the almost cooked meat, and broil a final minute.

Incidentally, if you are tempted to leave out the garlic listed in this recipe, Think twice. You should first know that the fresh ginger also used will deodorize this pungent herb and make it far less antisocial but still packed with flavor.

5 pounds tart crisp apples
1 large mild purple onion
1 large clove garlic
1 small slice fresh green ginger
4 cups dark brown sugar
6 cups vinegar
2 pounds seedless raisins
1 tablespoon salt
1 tablespoon white mustard seed
1 tablespoon curry powder
1 teaspoon cinnamon

Peel, core, and chop the apples. Peel and chop the onion, mince the garlic, and chop fine the ginger.

Put all ingredients in a large, deep preserving kettle. Stir over moderate heat until sugar has dissolved, then let boil gently for about 45 minutes to an hour, or until thick, fragrant, and dark.

Ladle into clean hot jars and seal.

Makes about 8 half-pints.

Alice Conroy's Special Chutney

This is a spicy-hot chutney, but you can cut down on the "hot" if you want to by using half the number of red peppers. Either way—hot or mild—the flavor, texture, and color of this chutney will all score high with chutney "aficionados." Alice adapted this recipe from a basic one, changing both the method of preparation (making it easier) and the seasoning (making it better).

1 cup malt vinegar

6 or 8 fresh hot red peppers

1 large yellow onion

1 large clove of garlic

3 large mangoes

6 limes

½ cup chopped fresh green
  ginger root

¾ cup chopped preserved ginger

½ cup syrup from preserved ginger

3 cups dark brown sugar

1 teaspoon salt

1 teaspoon dry mustard

1 1-inch stick cinnamon,
  broken up

1 drop each red, green, and
  yellow food coloring

Put the vinegar with the peppers in an electric blender and blend until smooth. Pour this into the preserving kettle and set aside while you prepare the vegetables and fruit.

Peel and chop the onion and garlic. Peel the mangoes. Cut the fruit into narrow strips about ½ inch thick and 2 inches long, discarding seed. Squeeze the limes. Lastly, chop and measure the fresh ginger. Everything ready, add the chopped onion and garlic, the mango strips, the lime juice, and all remaining ingredients except food coloring to the vinegar in the preserving kettle. Bring to a boil, lower heat, cover, and let simmer for about 15 minutes. Let stand uncovered at room temperature until cool, then cover and refrigerate overnight.

Next day cook gently until very thick, about 1 hour. Stir in food coloring.

Let chutney stand to plump up the fruit. Stir occasionally. When cool, ladle into clean hot jars.

Makes 4 pint jars.

Mango Chutney from the Oberoi Grand Hotel

4 pounds mangoes
2 quarts white vinegar
4 cups light brown sugar, packed down
1 lime, chopped
1 large onion, peeled and chopped
1 clove garlic, peeled and minced
2 cups raisins
¼ cup mustard seed
2 red peppers, crumbled
2 teaspoons salt
½ teaspoon cloves
2 cups preserved ginger, chopped
Syrup from preserved ginger

Peel the mangoes, and cut the fruit into strips about ½ inch wide and 3 inches long, discarding seeds. Place in a large pot and add 1 quart of the vinegar. Bring to a boil, then lower the heat and let simmer for 30 minutes. Drain, reserving 1 cup of the vinegar.

As soon as you have the mango strips and vinegar

on the stove, combine the remaining vinegar and the sugar in the preserving pot and place over medium heat. Stir until the sugar has dissolved, then let simmer for 30 minutes. Add the drained mango strips, the reserved vinegar, and all the remaining ingredients except the preserved ginger and ginger syrup. Now let this boil gently for 30 to 45 minutes, or until quite thick. Stir often to prevent sticking. Add the chopped ginger and ginger syrup and continue to cook for a final 10 minutes.

Take the chutney from the stove and let stand at room temperature for 4 to 5 hours. This really does improve the flavor. Stir it from time to time. Return the pot to the heat, bring to a full boil, and boil for about 5 minutes. Stir often and stay with it because at this point the chutney is very apt to stick.

Ladle into clean hot jars and seal.

Makes 8 to 9 half-pint jars.

Peach Chutney

3 ounces green ginger root
4 cups cider vinegar
3 cups dark brown sugar, packed down
1 teaspoon ginger
1 teaspoon cinnamon
1 teaspoon allspice
2 tart apples
1 large mild purple onion
1 clove garlic
4 pounds firm but ripe peaches
1 cup seedless raisins
1 drop each yellow, green, and red food coloring

Dice the ginger root and put it in the preserving kettle. Add the vinegar, sugar, and spices. Stir over medium heat until sugar dissolves, then let simmer until thick as honey, about 20 minutes.

While the syrup cooks, prepare the remaining ingredients.

Peel, core, and coarsely chop the apples. Peel the onion and garlic and mince these very fine. Peel the peaches and cut them into slices about ¼ inch thick. Crack 4 of the peach pits and extract the seed from each. Place them in a small saucepan, cover with water, and let simmer for about 5 minutes. Drain, slip off the brown skins, and chop fine.

Add apples, onion, peaches, chopped peach seeds, and raisins to the simmering syrup and cook until fruit is tender and mixture is thick.

Remove from heat and stir in food coloring. This combination of colors will give you a deep, rich brown chutney.

Ladle into clean hot jars and seal.

Makes about 6 pints.

Pineapple Chutney

This chutney has a number of good things to recommend it. First, all the ingredients are available year-round at your supermarket, so you can make it midwinter or any time. Second, it's inexpensive; large cans of pineapple can often be picked up at a bargain-sale price. Third, it's quick and easy to make. It can be done at the same time you prepare the curry it's to be served with. Lastly—but really most important—it's rich, dark, spicy sweet, and hot. In other words, it's delicious. And I think you will like it.

1 large juicy lemon

1 1-pound 13-ounce can sliced pineapple in syrup

1 clove garlic

2 cups brown sugar, packed down

1¼ cups cider vinegar

1½ cups seedless raisins

1½ cups tiny black currants

1 8-ounce package broken walnuts

½ cup chopped candied or preserved ginger

½ teaspoon salt

¼ teaspoon black pepper

¼ teaspoon crushed red pepper

4 whole cloves

½ teaspoon allspice

Pare off the yellow part of the lemon peel and cut it into the thinnest possible strips. I make short work of this by using my thinnest, sharpest sewing scissors instead of a chopping board and knife. Put the strips in a small pan, cover with water, and let simmer for about 30 minutes. Drain.

Next cut the now white lemon into paper-thin slices and cut each slice into four wedges. Remove and discard seeds. Then cut sliced pineapple into slivers and peel the garlic.

Combine all ingredients in a large, deep saucepan. Place over medium heat and bring to a full boil and boil for about 25 minutes or until as thick as you like it.

Remove the pan from the heat. Fish out and discard the garlic and cloves. Then ladle your chutney into clean hot jars and seal.

Makes only 2 or 3 pint jars, but you can double the recipe with only a little extra work.

To Speak of
Spiced and Brandied Fruit

I fell in love with spiced and brandied fruits in Paris. I had just left Fauchon, that temple of gastronomy in the Place de la Madeleine, still dizzy with the sheer opulence of the rows of pâtés, truffles, and cheeses, of fruits and vegetables so beautiful they should be painted instead of eaten, and there suddenly was Tanrades'. Number 18 Rue Vignon read a neatly polished brass plate, but it was the window that held me fascinated even as it began to rain.

There were rows of crystallized fruit, slices of pineapple, oranges and lemons, beautiful huge cherries, whole citrons, great jars of peaches, of plums. Quite by accident I had discovered the oldest and most famous confiture shop in Paris. For two hundred years Tanrades has been making the finest crystallized, spiced, and brandied fruit in France. I bought all I could carry and managed to get them home, cheerfully paying for the extra weight on the plane.

I used every jar. Spiced peaches accompanied even

lowly meat loaf, the syrup was used to baste a ham, brandied cherries were flamed over ice cream, crystallized orange peel was crumbled into cakes and puddings. Every last bite vanished and I had become thoroughly spoiled.

Not having the wherewithal for another trip to Paris, I resolved to duplicate every delicious fruit in my own kitchen, and I did, for I found that Tanrades' secret was simple. Use the best fruit, good brandy and spices, and pure sugar. Add a little care and the results are fantastically good.

Spicy Red Crab Apples

5 pounds crab apples
Water to cover
5 cups sugar
2 tablespoons red cinnamon
   candy
1½ cups cider vinegar
6 or 8 whole cloves
1 thin slice ginger root,
   crushed

Don't peel the crab apples but do wash each one thoroughly. It's a rare apple these days that has not been sprayed with something. Remove only the blossom ends.

Put the apples in your widest, largest pan and add only enough water to cover. Bring to a full boil and then lower heat and let simmer gently for about 10 minutes. Drain apples and reserve 1½ cups liquid. Place liquid with remaining ingredients in the preserving kettle and stir over medium heat until sugar dissolves. Let boil for 5 minutes, then add crab apples. Lower heat and let simmer very gently until they are tender.

Remove the crab apples from the syrup with a slotted spoon and place them in clean hot wide-mouth jars. Cover the jars to keep the apples hot.

Boil syrup hard for 2 or 3 minutes, then pour into the jars to ¼ inch from the top and seal.

Makes 5 to 6 pints.

The leftover syrup can be used in any number of ways. It's a wonderful ham glaze or a baste for sweet potatoes or acorn squash.

Spiced Banana Chunks

4 cups sugar
1 cup white wine vinegar
3 pounds firm ripe bananas
2 1-inch sticks cinnamon,
    broken up
6 whole cloves
1 cup seedless raisins
1 cup broken walnuts

Place sugar and vinegar in a large, deep saucepan and bring to a boil. Lower heat and let simmer for about 15 minutes.

Peel the bananas, cut them into thick slices, and add them to the syrup. Add remaining ingredients and let cook until the bananas can be easily pierced with a food pick or wooden skewer.

Ladle into jars and seal.

Makes about 4 pints.

Kümmel Cherries

5 pints cherries
4 cups white wine vinegar
8 whole cloves
1 2-inch stick of cinnamon
Small pieces of whole ginger
8 cups sugar

A great French chef once told me that the way food looks is second only to the way it tastes. Picture kümmel cherries in a clear crystal bowl on a crystal plate with a silver spoon, next to a crisp and golden roasted turkey.

You must stone the cherries carefully to keep the fruit whole, but after this job the work is more a matter of time than effort. Put the pitted cherries in a large non-metal bowl.

Place the vinegar and spices in an enamel pan and bring to a boil over medium heat. Lower heat and let simmer for 15 minutes. Then let stand at room temperature until cool. Strain and pour over cherries. Let stand overnight.

Next morning drain off the vinegar and pour the sugar over the cherries.

Cover the bowl and let stand for 8 days, stirring each day.

Fill the clean hot jars to the brim with cherries and liquid. Seal.

Makes about 8 half-pint jars.

Brandied Fruit

This recipe begins with a bottle of fine cognac, the best your budget permits. You need a big, old-fashioned stoneware crock too—one with a good heavy lid. A 3-quart size is just about right.

1 quart fine cognac or
   best possible brandy
Grated rind of one orange
Grated rind of one lemon
Grated rind of one lime
1 stick cinnamon
12 whole cloves
6 whole allspice
1 quart ripe strawberries
4 cups sugar
Sweet cherries, stemmed
Ripe peaches, peeled and
   quartered with pits
Ripe pineapple, peeled and
   quartered and cut into cubes
Blackberries, raspberries, and grapes
Sugar

Wash and rinse the crock thoroughly and wipe it dry, especially the insides. Pour in the cognac and add the grated rinds, whole spices, strawberries, and sugar. Place a plate directly over the berries to hold them down in the cognac. Cover the crock tightly and leave in a cool place for 1 week.

Add cherries, peaches, pineapple, blackberries, raspberries, and grapes as they become available during the season. At the same time add an equal amount of sugar. Keep fruit submerged in cognac by weighing it down with the plate.

When the last fruit is added, cover the crock very tightly and let stand in a cool place for 3 months. Then it can be packed in clean jars and sealed for gift-giving or simply kept in the crock in a cool place to make special any number of desserts.

New Orleans Spiced Figs

This is an old family recipe that has always been a favorite of mine. In an old courtyard in the French quarter of New Orleans we ate these figs for breakfast with buttermilk biscuits hot from the oven and spread with sweet butter. The biscuits had top crusts that were crisp as toasted crackers, flaky layers inside that literally melted in your mouth, and bottom crusts just firm enough to spread with soft butter and top with figs. It's hard to imagine anything that tasted better.

I have never been able to quite duplicate those biscuits—perhaps I lack a touch that is light enough—but my spiced figs are exactly as I remember them—plump and juicy but firm and fresh-tasting, in a not-too-sweet syrup that's good enough to serve alone after the figs are long gone.

5 quarts ripe figs
2 quarts water, approximately
2 tablespoons salt
2 tablespoons alum
4 cups sugar
1 pint cider vinegar
1 tablespoon cloves
2 cinnamon sticks, broken up

Don't peel the figs or remove the stems, just wash quickly under cold running water. Place them in a non-metal bowl and cover with about 2 quarts of water to which you have added the salt. Let stand overnight. Drain and blot dry with paper towels.

Put the alum in a large pot and cover with about 1 cup water. Place over moderate heat and stir until dissolved. Add the figs, then pour in enough water to cover them. Bring to a full boil, then immediately re-move the pot from the stove. Drain the figs into a large colander and rinse thoroughly under cold running water. All of the alum must be washed away. Blot them dry with paper towels.

Combine the sugar, vinegar, and spices in the pre-serving kettle and stir over moderate heat until the sugar has dissolved. Bring to a gentle boil and let boil for 5 minutes. Add the figs and continue to boil for about 30 minutes, or until syrup has thickened.

Remove the hot figs from the syrup with a slotted spoon and place them in clean hot jars. Pack loosely. When all the jars have been filled, bring the syrup to a boil once again. Then pour into the jars to ¼ inch of the top and seal.

Makes 8 to 10 half-pint jars.

Spiced Kumquats

Preserved kumquats are the perfect dessert after a Chinese dinner, or any dinner for that matter, served in dessert bowls with a little of the syrup. Great too with baked ham instead of the usual spiced peaches.

Commercially prepared, they are in the luxury food class, but you can make them with in-season fruit for very little money.

Most recipes simply boil the fruit in a sugar syrup, but a Chinese cook in San Francisco gave me a way to prepare them that is ever so much better. They are boiled first in lemon water then cooked with sugar and added spices.

1 quart kumquats
1 lemon
1 teaspoon salt
1 pound sugar
1 cup water
Cloves
Stick cinnamon

Wash kumquats thoroughly. Cut two slight gashes at right angles across the blossom ends. Cut the lemon into thin slices. Place kumquats and lemon in a large pot and cover with water. Add salt and bring to a full boil. Drain and cover with fresh unsalted water and again bring to a full boil. Lower heat and let simmer until a food pick will pierce the skins easily. Let stand overnight. Drain and stick a clove in each kumquat.

Place the sugar and water in a preserving kettle. Stir over low heat until the sugar has dissolved. Add the kumquats and 2 or 3 broken-up sticks of cinnamon. Cover the pot and let the fruit simmer for about 1 hour or until it appears transparent. Remove pot from heat and let stand covered until the syrup is cool. This takes several hours.

Using a slotted spoon, loosely fill very clean half-pint jars with kumquats. Put a piece of the cinnamon in each jar.

When the jars have been filled, reheat the syrup to boiling and fill the jars to ¼ inch of top. Seal.

Makes 4 half-pint jars with some syrup left over, which you can use for pancakes or waffles—lovely!

Brandied Orange Slices

This is an elegant preserve, especially nice to serve with roast pork or veal. Try it too as a dessert with ice cream or as a topping for little custard tarts.

8 thick-skinned California
  oranges
Water
1 cup white wine vinegar
4 cups sugar
2 teaspoons cassia buds
½ teaspoon oil of cloves
1 cup brandy

Slice oranges about ¼ inch thick and then cut each slice in half. Remove and discard seeds. Place in a saucepan and cover with water. Let simmer over moderate heat until the skins are tender, about 1 hour. Drain.

Put the vinegar, sugar, and spices in a preserving kettle and bring to a boil. Let boil for 5 minutes. Add orange slices, lower heat, and let simmer until slices are well glazed.

Use a spatula or slotted spoon to pack the slices into 3 pint jars. They look their best with all the skin sides against the side of the jar.

Add the brandy to the hot syrup and ladle it over the orange slices, filling the jars to the brim. Seal.

Brandied Peaches

An elegant gift for Christmas-giving is a big fat jar of brandied peaches. Tied with shiny red ribbon and filled with tipsy fruit, it looks so generous and extravagant—though it's not, when put up in midsummer with bargain-priced peaches, then left to leisurely make its own brandy.

Exact quantities can't be given because this depends on the size and ripeness of the peaches, but for each half-gallon jar you will need approximately:

6 pounds peaches (Look for
    small, ripe but not overripe,
    unblemished fruit.)
1 teaspoon ginger (optional)
2 pounds sugar
24 raisins

Plunge peaches into boiling water, then hold briefly under cold water, and the skins will slip off easily.

Stir ginger into sugar.

Cover the bottom of a wide-mouth, half-gallon, screw-top glass jar with a layer of sugar to a depth of about ½ inch. Now add a layer of peaches and cover them with a second layer of sugar, making sure to fill in all the crevices between the fruit. Add a few raisins and repeat with successive layers of peaches, sugar, and raisins, ending with sugar, until the jar is full to the brim.

Cover the jar with paper towels or a clean cloth and tie down with string or use a rubber band to hold it in place.

Leave the jar overnight at room temperature. Next

morning open it and you will find that the peaches have shrunk to about half their former size.

Add more peaches and sugar and refill the jar. Keep this up for a week or until the jar remains full after standing overnight.

Cover the top of the jar with foil and hold in place with string or a rubber band. Punch 2 tiny holes in the foil with a food pick and leave for 6 weeks. At the end of that time remove the foil, put the lid on the jar, screw tight, and let stand in a cool, dark place for 6 months.

Caramel Peaches

This recipe uses a splendid flavor combination—the sweet, tart taste of fresh peaches teams beautifully with the caramel flavor of brown sugar.

4 to 5 pounds medium ripe
    peaches (enough to make
    8 cups peeled and sliced
    peaches)
⅓ cup cognac or good brandy
2 cups light brown sugar
4 cups white sugar

Peel, pit, and slice peaches. Not too thin—¼ inch is about right.

Put peaches, brandy, brown sugar, and white sugar in a preserving kettle. Bring slowly to a boil, stirring constantly until sugar dissolves. Let simmer, stirring frequently, until peach slices are translucent and syrup is thick.

Remove from heat and ladle immediately into clean hot jars. Fill to within ¼ inch of top. Seal.

Makes 6 or 7 half-pint jars.

Whisky Peaches

The perfect accompaniment to baked ham. Companionable too with fried chicken or roast duck. Great as dessert with ice cream, sour cream, or sweetened whipped cream. Use the best fruit available; these are show-off preserves.

1 lemon

3 pounds small, firm, ripe
  peaches

1 quart best-quality whisky

4 cups sugar

1 tablespoon whole cloves

With a sharp little knife or one of those handy little potato parers, cut the yellow outer peel from the lemon and cut it into thin strips about 1 inch long. Squeeze the lemon juice.

Plunge the peaches into boiling water for a half minute, then slip off their skins. Cool them quickly under cold running water if you must, but the skins will come off much more easily if you peel them as hot as your hands can tolerate.

As soon as each peach is peeled, put it in a large pan of cold water to which you have added the lemon juice. This will keep them from turning brown.

Put the whisky, sugar, lemon peel, and cloves in your preserving kettle and stir over medium heat until the sugar has dissolved. Add the peaches and let simmer until tender but not falling apart. Time depends on the ripeness of the peaches, and some will be tender before others, but it's usually only about 20 minutes.

With a slotted spoon remove each peach when tender from the syrup and put into wide-mouth jars. Then let the syrup simmer about 15 minutes longer or until thick. Pour syrup over the peaches to ¼ inch of top of jars.

If there is not enough syrup to cover all the peaches, add more whisky. Seal the jars tightly and invert them for a few minutes. When cool, store in a dark place for a few weeks before using.

Makes 3 quarts.

Spiced Seckel Pears

6 pounds Seckel pears
2 tablespoons salt
6 cups sugar
4 cups cider vinegar
2 cups water
3 tablespoons whole cloves
6 or 8 2-inch cinnamon sticks,
   broken up

Peel the pears but leave the stems on and don't core them. As soon as each pear is peeled, drop it into a large pot of water to which you have added the salt.

When all the pears are peeled, put the pot over high heat and bring to a boil. Lower heat and let simmer for 10 minutes. Drain.

While pears parboil, combine sugar, vinegar, water, and spices in the preserving kettle. Stir over medium heat until sugar dissolves. Let boil hard for 5 minutes, then add parboiled pears and cook at just above simmering until tender enough to pierce easily with a small knife.

Take the kettle from the heat and remove the pears with a slotted spoon and pack them into clean, hot, wide-mouth jars. Add a clove or two and a bit of cinnamon stick to each jar. Cover the jars to keep the pears warm, but don't seal them at this point.

Boil the syrup hard for about 25 minutes, then pour it boiling hot over the pears, filling each jar to ¼ inch of the top. Seal.

Makes about 4 to 6 quarts.

Brandied Plums

4 pounds large ripe plums
1 quart best-quality brandy
6 cups sugar

Select the largest possible plums. They should be soft and quite ripe. Wipe each plum clean with a damp cloth, then prick in several places with the tines of a fork. The old recipe, given to me by a lady in Summerville, South Carolina, says to use a silver fork, but my silver-plated one did just as well.

Place the plums in a large glass jar or a stoneware crock and pour the brandy over them. Cover with several thicknesses of cheesecloth and tie it tautly in place with string or secure with a large rubber band. Let stand in a cool but dry and dark place for 10 days.

Now put the sugar in a large preserving pot and dump the plums and brandy over it. When the juices from the fruit have saturated the sugar, you are ready to put the pot on the stove. Cook over low heat until the sugar dissolves, stirring often. Then let boil gently for 25 to 30 minutes, stirring occasionally at first, then quite often to prevent scorching. Remove from heat and ladle into clean hot jars and seal.

Makes about 6 half-pint jars.

Pompion
SPICED PUMPKIN CHIPS

Pumpkins always bring to mind crisp and cool New England in September and "pumpkins on the frosty vine," but I don't think many people in that part of the country make preserves of pumpkins. I certainly have never seen any. Yet pompion, as it's named in old southern cookbooks, is as delicious a preserve as I've eaten.

This is the simplest of preserves to prepare, but there are many variations. The best one I found has a sharp, lemony flavor counterbalanced by spicy preserved ginger.

1 firm, medium-sized pumpkin
  weighing about 5 pounds (to
  make about 4 pounds pumpkin
  chips)
3 lemons
3 oranges
4 pounds sugar
1 8-ounce jar preserved ginger

Peel the pumpkin and cut it into strips, discarding seed and pulp. Cut strips into small thin chips.

Squeeze juice from lemons and oranges. Discard seeds. Cut rind into thin, thin slivers. Put slivers in plastic bag and refrigerate until ready to use.

Combine juices, pumpkin chips, and sugar in a deep non-metal bowl. Stir and lift the chips so that the sugar is evenly distributed. Cover and refrigerate 8 to 12 hours. Obviously it's a good idea to do this late in the afternoon so you can continue in the morning.

Transfer mixture to preserving kettle. Place over low heat and stir until the liquid made by the pumpkin and sugar starts to boil. Lower heat and let simmer for about 1 hour, stirring often to prevent scorching. Add the reserved lemon and orange skin slivers and continue to cook, stirring often, until chips appear transparent and syrup is quite thick. Add preserved ginger and its syrup during the last 10 minutes of cooking. (Total cooking time: approximately 2 hours.)

Ladle into clean hot jars, making sure each jar gets its share of lemon and orange strips as well as of ginger.

Makes about 9 half-pint jars.

Note: It's best to be in the kitchen while this preserve is on the stove because it does require watching. I go on to something else and keep a long-handled spoon on a saucer nearby to stir the chips up from the bottom of the pot each time I take a look at how they are progressing.

Annabelle's Gingered Watermelon-Rind Chips

Watermelon-rind preserves are my all-time favorite, but I never used to like making them. Every recipe I tried was so complicated and time-consuming. There was always much soaking and draining and putting the chopped rind into the syrup and taking it out again. Every time I got halfway into the making I swore it would be the last, until Annabelle Major gave me her recipe. The recipe is relatively simple. You do have to chop up the rind, but the rest is one-two-three simple, and the preserves are positively grand. Besides, there's the bonus of all that juicy pink fruit to chill and eat. I particularly admire it for breakfast.

1 4½- to 5-pound thick-skinned watermelon
5 pounds sugar (11¼ cups)
3 lemons
1 1-pound jar preserved ginger

Quarter the melon and scoop out the red part. With a sharp knife cut away the green skin and any remaining pink fruit. Cut the white rind into thin (about ½ inch) strips. Cut the strips into neat, even ½-inch cubes. This takes patience, but it's worth the trouble because the resulting preserves will cook faster and more evenly and will also look more elegant in the jars.

Put the diced rind in a large non-metal bowl. The bowl should be no more than half full. If you do not have one that is sufficiently large, use two smaller ones because the rind swells until almost double in bulk and forms a liquid that can overflow.

Dump the sugar over the rind.

Don't mix yet. Just set the bowl aside. Cut the lemons in half and squeeze out the juice. Discard the seeds and sprinkle the juice over the sugar. (To get plenty of juice from the lemons roll them on your chopping board, pressing down hard with the palm of your hand. They will become soft and much more juicy in about 1 minute.)

Cut the lemon rinds into thin strips about 1 inch long, leaving the pulp attached. Add this to the bowl.

Using two big wooden spoons, lift and toss the rind and sugar as you would a green salad, only much more carefully to avoid spilling sugar all over your kitchen counter.

When everything is thoroughly blended, cover the bowl and let stand 8 hours or overnight. (You may refrigerate if you wish, but bring to room temperature before proceeding.)

When you are ready to continue, first drain and dice the preserved ginger, reserving the liquid. Then transfer the rind and sugar mixture to a large preserving kettle. Place over medium heat and bring to a boil. Lower heat and add the diced ginger and the ginger liquid. Let simmer until the rind is soft and the syrup is very thick. Ladle into clean hot jars and seal.

Makes about one dozen half-pint jars.

Note: These preserves must mellow a bit. They are at their best after about 2 months on a cool dark shelf.

Gifts from
Your Oven

"Four and twenty black birds
    Baked in a pie.
When the pie was opened,
    The birds began to sing;
Was not that a dainty dish,
    To set before a king?"

You may not want to send a pie of singing blackbirds to your nearest and dearest, but there is little else as welcome as a homemade cake or a box of fresh cookies, especially today when the small corner bakery is fast disappearing under the onslaught of mass-produced supermarket desserts that bear no resemblance to the real butter and egg cakes and cookies you make in your own kitchen.

If the idea of sending your more sophisticated friends a homemade cake turns you off, stop and think for a moment. Homemade doesn't mean corny, far from it; homemade means creative. A fruit cake aged in real cognac can be the most exciting of Christmas

101

presents. As for birthdays, I've never known anyone young or old who wasn't thrilled by an imaginative birthday cake made just for them.

The difference between so-so and superb is up to you.

Use your imagination to select the right gift for the right person just as you would if you were selecting a present in a store. For example, if you have an older woman friend on your list who is devoted to her afternoon tea, an applesauce cake would probably delight her. It will keep for weeks in the refrigerator and a thin slice of it is the perfect teatime accompaniment. Add a tin of fine imported tea bags and you have the super perfect present.

Try giving birthday cakes a fresh new look and taste with some interesting colors and flavors, perhaps a mint jelly filling and pale green frosting, the top of the cake decorated with green candy leaves. Or try a chocolate cake for a man iced with coffee frosting then sprinkled with instant coffee. My own favorite birthday cake is frosted in a pretty pastel then decorated with fresh flowers.

Homemade cookies can become very special too. Again think of the lucky recipient: A box of Langues de Chats can go to the most elegant couple on your list; a large family would love a big tin of assorted sugar cookies; while your bachelor friends will welcome a supply of cheese straws for their cocktail parties.

If you like to bake, gifts from your oven can be a delight to give and to receive.

All of the recipes here have been "gift tested," and the only adverse comment I have ever received was that "it disappeared so fast." Some are very simple

and quick to make and some take a bit more "doing," but none are difficult or tricky and none require elaborate equipment.

Happy baking.

All About Equipment

You probably have all of the equipment needed for most baking, but just to be sure here's a checklist of essentials.

> 2 large mixing bowls
> Set of smaller bowls
> Measuring cups
> Measuring spoons
> 2 long-handled wooden spoons
> French wire whisk (indispensable for me)
> 3 round layer cake tins
> 2 generous-size cookie sheets
> Spring-form angel food or sponge cake pan
> 2 loaf pans
> 2 cake racks
> Flour sifter
> Sharp chopping knife
> Chopping board

All of the above are necessities, however I hasten to add that both an electric blender and mixer are handy to have.

Special Tips

The number one rule is to have all ingredients at room temperature, otherwise you simply cannot turn out really good cakes, cookies, or rolls. This means allowing at least 2 hours in a warm room for refrigerated eggs, milk, butter, etc. If eggs are to be separated, separate them while still cold.

Before you begin, read over the recipe carefully and assemble your ingredients.

Measure carefully, using accurate measuring cups and spoons, and always sift flour before measuring for cakes and cookies.

Brown sugar must be packed firmly into measuring cup and be free from lumps. To keep brown sugar soft wrap the box tightly in foil and store in the refrigerator.

For delicate cakes, try using super fine sugar if it is available in your area.

Butter cakes require thorough creaming of the butter and sugar. The mixture should be very light and fluffy with no trace of undissolved sugar.

If the recipe calls for well-beaten egg yolks, beat with a wire whisk until thick and lemon colored. You can beat egg yolks with an electric mixer but your cake will not be as light.

Egg whites should always be beaten with a whisk. A rotary beater, electric or not, simply does not allow enough air to be beaten into the whites. Beaten egg whites should always be carefully folded into batter.

Cakes should be well beaten after the egg yolks have been added, but should be mixed only enough to blend after the addition of flour. Overbeating at this time will make the cake dry and coarse.

Always preheat the oven for any baked goods. This assures even cooking and proper rising.

Remove cakes and cookies from their pans and cool on a wire rack before icing or decorating.

Sponge and angel food cakes should be inverted in the pan and allowed to hang on an inverted funnel or small heavy glass until completely cool.

Dough for rolled cookies should be chilled thoroughly before rolling otherwise more flour may have to be added. No one wants a "tough cookie."

Be sure to let yeast dough stand in warm, draft-free spot for rising. One good way to do this is to preheat the oven to warm then turn it off and allow it to cool to about 85°F. Cover the dough and place in the center of the oven. You can use paper towels to cover yeast dough but if you insist on using a dish towel make sure it is absolutely clean and free from soap.

Birthday Cakes

It's the filling and frosting that makes a birthday cake a special and very personal gift. Any good butter cake can be used, but this is my favorite. It's light but rich, high, and handsome enough to make a spectacular appearance when decorated with either plain white icing or icing plus all the trimmings.

The procedure for making the batter differs considerably from the usual butter cake, so do read over the directions carefully before you begin.

6 eggs
¼ pound (1 stick) butter
Vegetable oil, as needed
2¼ cups sifted cake flour
1½ cups sugar
3 teaspoons baking powder
½ teaspoon salt
1 tablespoon strained lemon
   juice, or substitute
   1 tablespoon brandy,
   2 teaspoons rum flavoring, or
   1 teaspoon vanilla
¾ cup water
½ teaspoon cream of tartar

Preheat oven to 350°F.

Separate the eggs while still cold, putting the yolks in one large bowl, the whites in another.

Bring all ingredients to room temperature.

Melt the butter over low heat. Let stand until room temperature, then carefully pour it into a measuring cup, leaving all the white sediment in the pan. Add sufficient vegetable oil to measure ½ cup liquid. Set aside.

Sift the flour, sugar, baking powder, and salt over the egg yolks. Add the butter and oil mixture, lemon juice, and water. Beat to a smooth batter.

Add the cream of tartar to the egg whites and beat until very stiff.

Beat the yolk batter briefly to eliminate air bubbles. Fold in the beaten egg whites a half at a time just until blended. Don't overmix.

Pour the batter into two 8-inch ungreased layer cake pans.

Bake for 35 minutes, or until cake will spring back when gently pressed with your finger.

Invert the pans and place each on the edges of 2 other pans. Let stand until the cakes are completely cool, about 1 hour. Loosen sides of cakes with a rubber spatula and invert cakes onto wire rack.

Let stand at least ½ hour, then split each layer horizontally to make 4 layers.

Spread with filling and frost with icing. Decorate "as your family pleases."

Easy One-Bowl Butter Cake

½ cup butter
1 cup sugar
2 eggs
1 teaspoon vanilla
1½ cups sifted cake flour
½ teaspoon salt
2½ teaspoons baking powder
½ cup milk

Have all ingredients at room temperature.
Preheat oven to 375°F.
Grease and flour two 9-inch layer cake pans.
Cream the butter and sugar until light as a feather, add eggs 1 at a time beating well after each addition. Add vanilla and beat again. Sift flour, salt, and baking powder together and add to butter mixture alternately with the milk. Mix only until blended. Pour into prepared pans and bake for 20 to 25 minutes. Remove cakes from pans and cool on a wire rack before icing.

Three-Part Chocolate Cake

PART ONE

2 cups sifted cake flour
½ teaspoon salt
1 teaspoon baking soda

PART TWO

½ cup sugar
½ cup cocoa
½ cup boiling water
 2 teaspoons vanilla

PART THREE

½ cup butter
 1 cup sugar
 2 eggs, well beaten
⅔ cup buttermilk

Preheat oven to 350°F.

Grease and flour two 8-inch layer cake pans.

Sift flour, salt, and baking soda together. Set aside.

Combine sugar, cocoa, and boiling water in a small saucepan. Cook over low heat stirring constantly until mixture is smooth and glossy. Add vanilla and blend. Cool thoroughly.

Cream butter and sugar together until very light and fluffy and no "grittiness" remains. Add beaten eggs and beat thoroughly. Add cooled chocolate mixture and beat again. Add flour mixture alternately with buttermilk, mixing just to blend. Turn batter into prepared pans and bake for 25 to 30 minutes.

Remove cakes from pans and cool on wire rack before icing.

Frostings and Fillings

NEVER-FAIL THICK WHITE ICING

This is a soft-on-the-inside crusty-on-the-outside icing.

2 egg whites
3 tablespoons cold water
2 cups granulated sugar
½ teaspoon cream of tartar
1 teaspoon flavoring (almond extract, strained lemon or lime juice, vanilla, artificial rum flavoring, instant powdered coffee, crème de cacao, etc.), or add to sugar before cooking 3 tablespoons any flavored gelatin.

Place all ingredients except flavoring (if using flavored gelatin add to sugar and mix well before proceeding) in top of double boiler. Beat with a wire whisk over simmering water until blended. Increase heat until water boils rapidly and beat constantly until very stiff, until frosting will stand in stiff peaks when beater is slowly removed. Place pan over cold water, add flavoring and beat until cool.

This is sufficient frosting and filling for 4 thin or 2 standard layers.

Suggestions for Decorating Cakes:
Sprinkle with fresh, packaged, or canned tinted coconut. To tint, dilute a few drops of food coloring in a teaspoon of water. Add to 1 cup coconut in a quart jar; cover and shake until evenly tinted.

Melt three 1-ounce bars of semisweet chocolate in top of double boiler over simmering water until partially melted. Remove from heat and stir until completely melted. Dribble over surface of iced cake.

Dust with slivered almonds, chopped walnuts or pecans.

Sprinkle with grated semisweet chocolate mixed with instant coffee.

Decorate with Ornamental Icing using a pastry tube and your own artistic touch.

ORNAMENTAL ICING

2 egg whites
Confectioner's sugar
½ teaspoon flavoring (vanilla
    extract, almond extract,
    imitation rum flavoring,
    or peppermint flavoring)
Food coloring

Beat egg whites until very frothy. Stir in 1 cup sifted confectioner's sugar. Add flavoring, blend, then add 1 or 2 drops food coloring, any color. Blend again and add more sugar, bit by bit, until frosting will hold its shape when piped through pastry tube.

CHOCOLATE FROSTING

½ cup (1 stick) butter
5 1-ounce squares
    unsweetened chocolate
¼ cup water
2½ cups confectioner's sugar
2 egg yolks

Bring butter to room temperature. Melt chocolate with water in top of double boiler over simmering water. Remove from heat.

Add sugar all at once and stir until mixture is smooth. Add egg yolks, 1 at a time, and beat well after each addition. Add butter one fourth at a time, beating well after each addition.

Makes sufficient frosting to cover top and sides of 2 standard or 4 thin layers.

CREAMY COCONUT CREAM-CHEESE FROSTING

½ cup butter, room temperature
1 cup packaged coconut
1 8-ounce package cream
   cheese, room temperature
4 to 5 cups sifted
   confectioner's sugar
2 tablespoons brandy, or milk
   mixed with ¼ teaspoon
   vanilla

Melt 2 tablespoons of the butter in a large skillet. Add coconut and stir over medium heat until golden brown.

In a large mixing bowl cream remaining butter with cream cheese. Add sugar a little at a time alternately with brandy or milk, beating well after each addition. Fold in coconut.

Makes sufficient frosting to cover 2 standard or 4 thin layers.

CRANBERRY FROSTING

½ cup cranberries
1 teaspoon grated lemon rind
½ cup water
2 cups sugar
2 egg whites

Put cranberries, lemon rind, and water in a small saucepan. Cook over medium heat until cranberries are quite soft (10 minutes). Cool to room temperature.

Combine cranberries, water, sugar, and egg whites in top of double boiler and beat over boiling water until soft peaks form when beater is slowly lifted from the pan.

Remove from heat and continue to beat until stiff enough to spread.

Makes enough frosting to frost 2 standard or 4 thin layers.

MOCHA FROSTING

¼ cup water
2 1-ounce squares
  unsweetened chocolate
2 teaspoons instant coffee
½ teaspoon vanilla
1 tablespoon butter, room
  temperature
About 1½ cups confectioner's
  sugar

Place water and chocolate in top of double boiler over simmering water until chocolate has melted. Stir in instant coffee, vanilla, and butter. Remove from heat and stir until butter has melted. Put 1 cup confectioner's sugar in a large mixing bowl. Add chocolate mixture and stir until smooth. Add enough additional sugar for frosting to come to spreading consistency.

Makes sufficient frosting to cover 2 standard or 4 thin cake layers.

BANANA FILLING

3 medium-size bananas
1 tablespoon lemon juice
2 tablespoons sugar

Mash bananas. Stir in lemon juice and sugar.
Makes about 1 cup.

STRAWBERRY FILLING

½ envelope unflavored gelatin
3 tablespoons water
½ cup heavy cream
½ cup sugar
1 cup mashed fresh strawberries

Sprinkle gelatin over water in a saucepan. Stir over low heat until dissolved.

Whip cream until stiff. Fold in sugar. Add dissolved gelatin to mashed strawberries and fold into whipped cream.

Makes about 2 cups.

LADY BALTIMORE FILLING

3 egg yolks
½ cup sugar
¼ cup butter
¼ cup cognac or other good
   brandy, or ¼ cup water plus
   1 teaspoon vanilla
¼ cup chopped candied cherries
¼ cup coarsely chopped
   seeded raisins
¼ cup coarsely chopped candied
   orange peel
¼ cup coarsely chopped walnuts

Place egg yolks in a large saucepan and beat until frothy. Add sugar and butter. Cook, stirring over

115

moderate heat, until sugar dissolves and mixture thickens.

Remove from heat. Add brandy or water and vanilla. Cool slightly then stir in fruits and nuts. Cool to room temperature before spreading between cake layers.

Makes about 2 cups.

APRICOT FILLING

- 1 cup dried apricots
- 1 tablespoon chopped lemon rind
- ¼ cup lemon juice
- ¾ cup sugar
- 3 tablespoons cornstarch

Put apricots in a large bowl and cover with boiling water. Let stand 1 hour. Transfer to a saucepan. Add additional water if necessary to cover apricots by 1 inch. Add lemon rind. Cook over moderate heat until apricots are very soft. Drain thoroughly.

Place drained apricots in the container of an electric blender or press through a food mill. Add the lemon juice and blend to a smooth puree.

Transfer to a saucepan. Add sugar and cornstarch. Place over medium heat and bring to a boil, stirring constantly. Stir for about 30 seconds.

Makes about 2 cups filling.

LEMON FILLING

3 egg yolks
¾ cup sugar
⅛ teaspoon salt
1 teaspoon grated lemon rind
2 teaspoons lemon juice
2 tablespoons cornstarch
¼ cup water
2 tablespoons butter

Beat egg yolks in top of double boiler until well blended. Add sugar, salt, lemon rind, lemon juice, cornstarch, and water. Stir to blend then place over boiling water and cook, stirring almost constantly, until thick. Stir in butter.

Makes about 1 cup.

Orange Chiffon Cake
with Orange Rum Glaze

1 orange
Water, if needed
6 eggs
½ cup safflower or corn oil
2 cups cake flour
1½ cups sugar
3 teaspoons baking powder
½ teaspoon salt
½ teaspoon cream of tartar

Preheat oven to 325°F. Put the rack in the lower half of the oven.

Grate the colored rind from the orange. Squeeze the juice. Measure juice and add sufficient water to make ¾ cup liquid.

Separate the eggs. Put the whites in your largest mixing bowl. To the yolks add the grated orange rind, the juice and water, and the oil. Stir to blend.

Sift the flour, sugar, baking powder, and salt into a third bowl. Make a well in the center and pour in the yolk mixture. Beat until very smooth.

Add cream of tartar to egg white and beat until very stiff. Fold gently into cake batter until just blended. Do not stir. Pour at once into an ungreased 10-inch tube pan. Bake in preheated oven for 1 hour or until cake springs back when lightly pressed with fingertips. Invert pan and place tube over a small heavy glass so that air can circulate around cake. Let stand until cool.

To remove the cake from the pan, loosen it from

the sides and tube with a table knife. Invert the pan and hit it gently against the table.

Place the cake on a platter and pour warm Rum Butter Glaze over surface.

RUM BUTTER GLAZE

½ cup light rum
2 tablespoons butter
2 cups sifted confectioner's sugar

Heat rum and butter until butter has melted. Pour over confectioner's sugar. Stir until smooth.

Bourbon Cake

3 cups water
2 cups white seedless raisins
½ pound butter, room temperature
1 cup bourbon
3½ cups all-purpose flour
2 cups chopped pecan meats
2 cups sugar
2 teaspoons baking soda
½ teaspoon nutmeg
½ teaspoon mace
¼ teaspoon allspice
¼ teaspoon ground ginger
2 eggs, well beaten

Preheat oven to 325°F.

Butter generously then flour lightly a 10-inch tube pan.

Put water with raisins in a saucepan and bring to a full boil over medium heat. Reduce heat and let simmer for 10 minutes. Add butter and stir until melted. Remove from heat and pour in bourbon. Let cool to lukewarm.

Sift ½ cup flour over pecan meats.

Combine remaining flour with sugar, spices, and baking soda. Sift into mixing bowl.

Pour raisin mixture over dry mixture and mix until well blended. Add beaten eggs. Blend, then fold in floured nuts.

Pour batter into prepared pan and bake in preheated oven for 1½ hours, or until cake springs back when lightly pressed with fingertips.

Invert pan and place tube over a small heavy glass so that air can circulate around cake.

When cool, turn out onto cake rack and let stand for 1 hour before packing or serving.

Brandied Almond Pound Cake

9 large eggs (not jumbo)
3 cups all-purpose flour
1 teaspoon baking powder
¼ teaspoon salt
1 pound (2 cups) butter
1 pound (2¼ cups) sugar
3 tablespoons ground almonds
3 tablespoons brandy plus about
   1 cup brandy for soaking
Confectioner's sugar

Preheat oven to 350°F.

Grease a 10-inch tube pan with vegetable shortening. Sprinkle lightly with flour. Rotate pan and coat inside evenly with flour. Shake out excess flour.

Separate eggs, placing whites in one large mixing bowl, yolks in another.

Sift the flour with baking powder and salt onto waxed paper; set aside.

Cream the butter with 1 cup of the sugar until very light and thoroughly blended.

Beat egg yolks with 1 cup of the sugar until very light and fluffy. Beat in the grated almonds and the 3 tablespoons brandy.

Beat egg whites until they just hold their shape. Then beat in remaining sugar.

Fold flour mixture into egg yolk mixture a quarter cup at a time blending only until combined. Fold in half of beaten egg whites at a time until just blended. Don't overmix.

Spoon batter into prepared pan.

Bake in preheated oven for 1 hour and 15 minutes, or until cake springs back when lightly pressed with fingertips.

Cool on rack for 15 minutes. Gently loosen sides with a spatula or knife. Turn out onto cake rack and cool.

Soak a length of cheesecloth in brandy. Wrap cake in soaked cloth then in foil. Store in refrigerator or in an airtight tin box, or if made more than 3 days ahead store in freezer.

Dust with confectioner's sugar just before wrapping as gift or just before serving.

Spicy Brown Sugar Pound Cake

   1 teaspoon lemon juice
   1 cup milk
  ½ cup butter
   2 cups light brown sugar,
     packed down
   4 eggs
   3 cups all-purpose flour
   1 cup chopped walnuts
  ¼ teaspoon salt
  ½ teaspoon baking soda
  ¼ teaspoon cinnamon
  ¼ teaspoon nutmeg
  ¼ teaspoon allspice
   1 teaspoon instant coffee

Preheat oven to 350°F.

Grease a 6-x-10-inch loaf pan generously with butter. Dust lightly with flour.

Stir lemon juice into milk. Set aside.

Cream butter with sugar. Add eggs, 1 at a time, beating well after each addition.

Mix ½ cup of the flour with the walnuts. Sprinkle with the salt.

Sift remaining flour with soda, spices, and coffee onto waxed paper. Add alternately with the milk to the butter mixture. Fold in nuts.

Pour into prepared pan and bake in preheated oven for 45 to 50 minutes. Turn out onto cake rack to cool.

Applesauce Cake

3 cups all-purpose flour
2 teaspoons baking soda
2 teaspoons cinnamon
½ teaspoon ground cloves
1 cup raisins, coarsely chopped
1 cup walnuts or pecans,
  coarsely chopped
1 cup dates, coarsely chopped
½ cup wheat germ
½ cup butter, room temperature
¾ cup brown sugar, firmly
  packed
2 eggs, well beaten
2 cups applesauce

Preheat oven to 325°F.

Grease and flour 2 6-x-10-inch loaf pans.

Sift together the flour, soda, cinnamon, and cloves. Mix half of the flour mixture with the raisins, walnuts, and dates; stir well to coat fruit and nuts evenly with flour. Combine remaining flour with wheat germ and blend well. In a separate bowl cream the butter with the sugar until very light and fluffy. Add eggs and beat until well blended. Add flour and wheat germ to the batter alternately with the applesauce, blending after each addition. Stir in fruit and nut mixture. Pour batter into prepared loaf pans and bake in preheated oven for 35 to 40 minutes. Turn out onto rack to cool.

Dutch Hustle Apple Cake

This recipe is an adaptation of one I received from the test kitchens of the makers of Fleishmans' Active Dry Yeast. It's quick and easy to prepare and truly delicious. Aptly named, I've often hustled it up to give, still warm from the oven, to new neighbors or as a new apartment or house gift.

4 crisp cooking apples or sufficient apples to make 2 cups apple slices

1 cup water

½ cup sugar

½ lemon cut into 2 wedges

2 tablespoons butter

2 tablespoons brown sugar

¼ teaspoon cinnamon

¼ teaspoon nutmeg

CAKE

1 to 1½ cups unsifted all-purpose flour

¼ cup sugar

½ teaspoon salt

1 package active dry yeast

3 tablespoons butter

½ cup water

1 large egg

Confectioner's sugar

To prepare topping:

Peel the apples cut into four wedges, remove core, and cut wedges into two or three fairly thick slices.

Combine water, sugar, and lemon wedges in a saucepan and stir over medium heat until sugar dissolves. Add apples slices and let simmer until tender but not mushy. Remove from heat and let cool in syrup while preparing cake.

Combine the two tablespoons butter with the brown sugar and spices. Work together with your fingers or with two knives until well blended. Set aside while preparing cake.

To prepare cake:

Grease an eight-inch-square baking pan.

In a large bowl, thoroughly mix ½ cup flour, the sugar, salt, and undissolved yeast.

Place butter and water in a small saucepan over medium heat until butter has melted and water is hot but not boiling. Gradually add this mixture to dry ingredients and beat for two minutes with an electric mixer at medium speed (or for 3 minutes by hand with a large wooden spoon) scraping the bowl occasionally. Add the egg and sufficient flour to make a soft batter —½ to ¾ cups.

Spread batter evenly in prepared pan.

Drain apples thoroughly and blot dry with paper toweling. Arrange apples over surface of batter, covering batter completely with apples. Sprinkle evenly with brown sugar and butter mixture. Cover, let rise in a warm place, free from drafts, until double in bulk, about one hour.

Preheat oven to 400°F.

Bake cake in preheated oven for 25-30 minutes. Remove from oven; let stand for ten minutes before removing from pan to wire rack. Can be served warm or cold.

Makes one 9-inch-square cake.

Orange Tea Bread

- 3 cups sifted whole wheat pastry flour (available at health food stores), or substitute all-purpose flour
- 1/3 cup sugar
- 2 teaspoons baking powder
- 1/2 teaspoon salt
- 1 teaspoon baking soda
- 1/2 cup chopped walnuts
- 2 eggs
- 1 1/2 cups orange marmalade
- 1 8-ounce carton vanilla yogurt

Grease 2 6-x-10-inch loaf pans.

Preheat oven to 350°F.

Sift flour, sugar, baking powder, salt, and baking soda into a large mixing bowl. Add walnuts and stir until blended.

In a second bowl beat eggs until blended. Stir in marmalade and then yogurt. Add egg mixture to flour mixture and mix just until blended and no dry flour appears.

Pour batter into greased loaf pans. Bake in preheated oven for 1 hour, or until cake springs back when lightly pressed with fingertips.

Let cool in pans on cake rack for 10 minutes. Gently loosen sides with a knife then invert and turn out onto cake rack. Cool completely then wrap in foil and store in freezer.

Makes 2 loaf cakes.

Banana Nut Bread

5 cups all-purpose flour
2 tablespoons baking powder
½ teaspoon salt
¼ teaspoon allspice
1 cup chopped walnuts
3 large bananas, peeled and chopped
⅔ cup milk
¼ cup cognac or brandy
2 eggs
2 cups sugar

Preheat oven to 350°F.

Grease and flour 2 10-x-6-inch loaf pans.

Sift flour, baking powder, salt, and allspice into mixing bowl. Add nuts and stir to blend.

Put bananas and milk in container of electric blender and blend until smooth. Pour over dry ingredients. Do not stir.

Put cognac, eggs, and sugar into container. Blend until smooth. Pour over bananas and milk. Stir to blend batter then beat for 1 to 2 minutes.

Pour into prepared loaf pans. Bake in preheated oven for 1 hour, or until firm. Let stand for 10 minutes, then turn out onto cake rack to cool.

Makes 2 loaves.

Note: Wrap in foil or plastic wrap and store in freezer. This bread can be sliced while frozen. Great when toasted and spread with cream cheese or butter. Keeps 3 to 6 months in the freezer.

"Christmas Fruitcake"

I start making fruit cakes early in November, ordering crystallized fruit from Bremen House, an old-fashioned German delicacy shop in New York, where they stock crystallized orange and lemon peel, pineapple, citron and cherries. These fruits do not contain preservatives and have a lovely fresh flavor that I find irresistible. Once my fruitcakes are made, I start soaking them with brandy. The longer they wait the better they are, so my best friends get the oldest cakes.

1½ pounds crystallized citron
1½ pounds crystallized pineapple
  1 pound crystallized orange peel
  1 pound crystallized lemon peel
  ½ pound crystallized cherries
  2 cups walnut meats
  4 cups flour
  4 teaspoons baking powder
  ¼ teaspoon salt
  2 cups butter (1 pound),
    room temperature
2½ cups brown sugar
    (firmly packed)
 10 eggs
  2 cups cognac or other
    good brandy
Additional cognac as needed

ABOUT BAKING PANS

I use four 8½ x 4½ x 2½-inch foil, loaf pans. The pans should be lightly greased with oil then lined with heavy brown paper, cut to fit the pan, allowing two extra inches at either end. You may use, instead, two 10 x 4-inch round, tube pans or the cakes can be baked in 6 (well greased with oil) one-pound shortening cans (start saving them in November), with a little batter left over to bake in paper muffin-pan cups for small "stocking gift" cakes.

ABOUT FRUITS, BATTER, AND BAKING

There are many fruit cakes on the market these days—very good ones, too—but I know of none that compares in flavor and texture to a homemade cake made with old-fashioned crystallized fruits that you chop yourself. True the chopping takes time, but this job can be done a day ahead and the next day's baking is one-two-three easy.

Using a wooden chopping board and a sharp cleaver, chop each fruit, one at a time, into very small pieces. This is easier if you dip your cleaver into hot water occasionally. As each fruit is chopped, place it in a large mixing bowl. Cover the bowl and refrigerate until about two hours before using.

When you are ready to proceed with your baking, bring the chopped fruit to room temperature.

Chop nuts and add to fruit. Then sprinkle one cup of the flour over the surface. With your hands, lift and mix the fruits and nuts until evenly covered with flour.

Sift remaining flour with the baking powder and salt and set aside.

Cream butter and sugar together until light and fluffy and no trace of grittiness remains. Add eggs one at a time, beating well after each addition. Add flour alternately with 1 cup of cognac, stirring well to blend. Add fruit and mix well but do not beat. Pour batter into prepared pans and bake in preheated oven for 2 hours.

Allow cakes to cool slightly before turning each out onto a clean piece of cheesecloth. Pour ¼ cup of remaining cognac over each cake, wrap in cheesecloth then in aluminum foil. Seal with Scotch tape and store in refrigerator or air-tight tin for a minimum of one month. Once a week, open foil and pour ¼ cup cognac over each cake. Reseal tightly.

Makes four 8½ x 4½ x 2½-inch loaf cakes or two 10-inch round cakes or six small, round cakes, plus about 6 cupcakes.

Panettone
ITALIAN CHRISTMAS BREAD

  2 envelopes dry granular yeast
¼ cup warm water
  1 cup milk
¼ pound (1 stick) butter
½ cup sugar
½ teaspoon salt
  2 eggs, well beaten
  4 cups sifted all-purpose flour
½ cup raisins
½ cup diced, mixed candied fruits

Bring all ingredients to room temperature.

Sprinkle yeast over warm water in a large mixing bowl.

In a large saucepan heat milk to scalding. Remove from heat and add butter, sugar, and salt. Stir until butter has melted. Cool to lukewarm, then stir in beaten eggs.

Add mixture to softened yeast in mixing bowl and stir until blended.

Add 3 cups of the flour a little at a time, beating well after each addition. Continue to beat after all flour has been added for a full minute or for 60 strokes.

Cover the bowl and let stand in a warm place free from drafts for about 1 hour, or until double in bulk.

Preheat oven to 350°F.

Grease a 12-inch loaf pan or a 10-inch bundt pan generously with vegetable shortening.

Mix remaining 1 cup of flour with the raisins and fruit and mix with your hands until evenly distributed.

Punch down dough and work in raisins and fruit with floured hands. Shape dough into a ball or loaf and place in bundt or loaf pan. Cover and let rise in a warm place until again double in bulk, about 1 hour.

Place in the preheated oven and bake until firm and nicely browned, about 45 minutes.

Let stand for about 15 minutes, then turn out onto a cake rack and cool completely before wrapping.

Danish Pecan Roll

 2 packages active dry yeast

¼ cup warm water

 1 cup milk

½ cup butter

⅓ cup sugar

½ teaspoon salt

 1 tablespoon light rum

 1 egg, well beaten

 4 cups unsifted all-purpose flour

 1 egg beaten with

 1 tablespoon water

Sprinkle yeast over warm water in a large mixing bowl.

Heat the milk until it begins to steam and bubbles appear around edge. Add butter, sugar, and salt.

Remove from heat and stir gently until butter has melted then cool to lukewarm (115° to 105°F.). Pour over yeast in mixing bowl and stir until blended.

Add rum and egg. Beat to blend then fold in 2 cups of the flour and beat with a wooden spoon until batter is smooth. Add remaining flour and with floured hands mix and knead until dough can be formed into a ball. Turn out onto floured board and knead until smooth and blisters form, about 5 minutes.

Place in a warm lightly greased bowl; turn greased side up. Cover and let rise in a warm place (85°F.) free from drafts until double in bulk, about 45 to 50 minutes.

Punch dough down and turn out onto a lightly floured board. Knead a few seconds then roll out into a rectangle about 20 x 12 inches. Spread with Filling, leaving a 1-inch margin. Roll up lengthwise and place seam-side down on a greased cookie sheet. Shape into a crescent. Cover and again put in a warm (85°F.) place away from drafts until double in bulk, about 1 hour.

Preheat oven to 375°F.

Brush surface of dough with egg and water mixture. Place in preheated oven and bake 20 to 25 minutes, or until golden in color.

Transfer to cake rack to cool.

FILLING

⅓ cup sugar
3 tablespoons butter
½ teaspoon cinnamon
1 cup finely chopped pecans
1 cup dark raisins
½ cup diced candied orange peel

Combine ingredients and blend well.

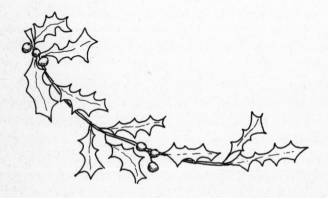

Christmas Buns

2 packages active dry yeast
¼ cup warm water
¾ cup milk
½ cup butter
½ cup sugar
½ teaspoon mace
¼ teaspoon cinnamon
⅛ teaspoon nutmeg
½ teaspoon salt
1 egg
4 cups sifted all-purpose flour
½ cup raisins
½ cup chopped pecans
½ cup finely chopped red and
   green candied fruit

Sprinkle yeast over water in a large mixing bowl.

Heat the milk to scalding. Add the butter, sugar, spices, and salt. Cool to lukewarm. Pour over softened yeast. Add the egg and beat until blended. Stir in 2½ cups of the flour. Beat for a full minute.

Add enough of the remaining flour to make a soft dough. Stir in raisins. Turn out onto a lightly floured board and knead for 10 minutes, or until smooth and elastic.

Place dough in a lightly buttered bowl. Turn to grease the surface. Cover and let rise in a warm place until double in bulk, about 1½ hours. Punch down and turn out on lightly floured board.

Press dough out lightly. Cover with the nuts and candied fruit. Knead to mix.

Pinch off pieces of dough and roll 3- or 4-inch

lengths about ½ inch thick. Tie into a loose knot
and place on a greased baking sheet.

Cover and let rise in a warm place for about 45
minutes, or until double in bulk.

Preheat oven to 400°F.

Bake the buns until firm and lightly browned, about
15 minutes.

Makes 18 to 24 small buns.

Pecan Rolls

ROLLS

¾ cup milk
½ cup sugar
 1 teaspoon salt
½ cup (1 stick) butter,
   very soft
⅓ cup lukewarm water
   (105°F. to 115°F.)
 2 packages active dry yeast
 3 eggs
5½ to 6½ cups unsifted
   all-purpose flour

TOPPING AND FILLING

Vegetable shortening
1½ cups dark cane syrup
2¼ cups chopped pecans
 3 tablespoons dark brown sugar
 6 tablespoons butter, very soft
¾ cup dark brown sugar

Bring all ingredients to room temperature.

Scald milk, stir in sugar, salt and butter. Cool to lukewarm.

Place warm water in a large *warm* mixing bowl. Sprinkle yeast over surface and stir until dissolved. Add lukewarm milk mixture, eggs, and three cups of flour. Beat until smooth. Stir in enough additional flour to make a stiff dough. Turn out onto a lightly floured board. Knead until smooth and elastic, about 8 to 10 minutes. Place in a warm, well-greased bowl, turning dough to grease top. Cover and let rise in a warm place, free from drafts, until double in bulk, about 1 hour.

Grease three 8-inch square pans generously with vegetable shortening. Pour about ½ cup syrup into each pan, covering bottom of pan completely. Sprinkle each with about ¾ cup chopped pecans then with 1 tablespoon brown sugar.

Punch dough down, divide into 3 equal pieces. Roll each piece into a rectangle about 9 x 7 inches. Spread each with softened margarine then sprinkle with brown sugar. Roll each up from the long side as for a jelly roll. Seal edges firmly. Cut into 1-inch slices. Place cut side up, in prepared pans. Cover, let rise in a warm place, free from drafts, until double in bulk, about 45 minutes.

Preheat oven to 400°F. Bake rolls in preheated oven for 25 to 30 minutes. Invert rolls onto plates to cool.

Makes about 26 rolls.

For gift giving:

Cool completely before wrapping rolls in plastic wrap and then in foil. Pack in single layers.

Cheese Straws

½ cup (¼ pound) unsalted
   butter, chilled
½ pound aged sharp cheddar
   cheese
2 cups flour
1 teaspoon cayenne pepper
1 large egg yolk, chilled
¼ cup ice water, more as needed

Preheat oven to 400°F.

Cut the butter into tiny slivers. Spread out on foil or a baking sheet and chill until very firm.

Grate the cheese into a large mixing bowl. Add flour, cayenne pepper, and chilled butter slivers. Use your hands to first toss and blend then rub mixture together until it resembles coarse corn meal. Work quickly and don't overmix or the butter will melt and make the dough oily.

Beat the egg yolk with the ice water only until blended then pour over the dry mixture. Work together with 2 forks to a soft dough. Add a little additional ice water if needed. Divide into 2 balls. Wrap in waxed paper and refrigerate until firm and well chilled, about 1 hour.

Working with 1 ball at a time, roll dough out on a lightly floured board. With a sharp knife trim the pastry to a neat rectangle then cut it crosswise into strips about 3 inches long and ½ inch wide. Use a spatula to transfer strips to an ungreased baking sheet.

Bake in preheated oven until firm to the touch, about 10 minutes. They should be a pale gold in color. Do not allow to brown. Transfer to a wire cake rack to cool.

Note: The unbaked straws may be frozen until firm, then packed in plastic bags as "gifts from your freezer."

Assorted Christmas Cookies

You use the same batter with a variety of toppings and decorations.

1 cup (½ pound) butter
2 cups sugar
2 eggs
3 cups flour
1 teaspoon baking powder
½ teaspoon cream of tartar
¼ teaspoon salt
Assorted toppings
About 3 tablespoons butter

Preheat to 400°F.

Grease cookie sheets.

Cream butter with sugar until light and fluffy. Beat in eggs 1 at a time.

Sift flour, baking powder, cream of tartar, and salt onto waxed paper. Add to butter-egg mixture a quarter at a time, blending after each addition.

With floured hands roll balls of dough about the size of a walnut. Place on greased cookie sheet 2 inches apart.

Spread out each of the toppings or commercially packaged red and green sugars you are going to use on a separate sheet of waxed paper. Put about 3 tablespoons of butter in a small bowl.

Dip a small glass or other flat-bottomed object first in butter then in topping and press down on cookie ball until about ⅛ inch thick. Repeat until all cookies have been covered with topping and flattened. Wipe bottom of glass clean each time you use a different topping.

Decorate cookies with nuts, cherry halves, chocolate shots, or gum drops.

Bake in preheated oven until edges are lightly browned, 8 to 10 minutes.

Makes about 6 dozen cookies.

MOCHA MIX TOPPING

3 1-ounce squares semisweet
  chocolate
1 tablespoon powdered instant
  coffee

Grate chocolate into a small bowl. Stir in instant coffee.

VANILLA SUGAR TOPPING

1 cup sugar
2 whole vanilla beans

Put sugar in a 1-pint mason jar. Coarse-chop vanilla beans then bury in sugar. Cover with lid. Let stand for about 1 week before using.

CINNAMON MIX TOPPING

1 cup sugar
1 tablespoon cinnamon

Place in small bowl and blend well.

Walnut halves
Pecan halves
Slivered almonds
Red and green candied cherries,
  chopped or cut in half
Chocolate shots
Chopped red and green
  gum drops

Fruit Cake Cookies

4 cups all-purpose flour
1 teaspoon nutmeg
1 teaspoon allspice
½ teaspoon ground ginger
3 teaspoons baking soda
2 cups chopped walnuts
½ cup chopped candied citron
1 cup chopped raisins
½ pound butter
2 cups brown sugar,
  packed down
4 eggs
1 cup light rum
2 tablespoons buttermilk

Preheat oven to 350°F.
  Grease cookie sheets.
  Sift flour with spices and soda onto waxed paper.
Mix 1 cup flour mixture with nuts and fruit.

Cream butter with sugar until light and fluffy. Add eggs 1 at a time and beat well after each addition.

Add rum and buttermilk alternately with flour and spice mixture. Blend well. Fold in nuts and fruits.

Drop by half teaspoonfuls onto greased baking sheet.

Bake in preheated oven until firm and edges begin to brown, about 10 minutes.

Makes about 4 dozen small cookies.

Almond Cookies

½ pound butter
2 cups all-purpose flour
1 cup sugar
½ teaspoon baking powder
Pinch of salt
1 egg
1 tablespoon ice water
¼ teaspoon almond extract
24 whole blanched almonds

Chill all ingredients.

Cut butter into small slivers.

Sift flour, sugar, baking powder, and salt into a large mixing bowl. Cut in butter with 2 knives or use your fingers to work it into the flour. Mixture should resemble coarse ground corn meal.

Beat the egg with the ice water and the almond extract until well blended.

Make a well in the center of the flour mixture and pour in the beaten egg.

Stir with a fork, then with your floured hands mix

and knead to a firm dough. Form into a ball and chill for 1 hour.

Preheat oven to 450°F.

Turn ball onto a lightly floured board and roll out to about ⅓ inch thickness. Cut with a small oval cookie cutter.

Place on a lightly greased baking sheet and press an almond into the center of each cookie.

Place in the preheated oven and bake for 10 minutes. Reduce heat to 250°F. and bake a final 20 minutes.

Cool on cake rack.

Makes 2 dozen small cookies.

Madeleines

You will need special madeleine pans for these little cakes. The cost is negligible however, and madeleines are easy to make. Although not expensive, they are not only rich-tasting but an elegant addition to any tea table.

    1 cup sweet butter
    1 cup cake flour
    ¾ teaspoon baking powder
    ¼ teaspoon salt
    3 large eggs
    ⅔ cup sugar
    ½ teaspoon almond extract
    ¼ cup finely grated almonds
    Confectioner's sugar

Preheat oven to 350°F.

Place butter in a small saucepan over moderate heat.

Brush 3 (12-cookie) madeleine pans lightly with melted butter. Set remaining melted butter aside to cool.

Sift flour with baking powder and salt onto waxed paper.

In a large mixing bowl beat the eggs with a wire whisk for 5 minutes. Add the sugar by tablespoonfuls, beating after each addition. Add the almond extract. Continue to beat an additional 5 minutes after all the sugar has been added. Gradually add in the flour mixture, folding it into the batter with an up and over motion. Fold in the grated almonds, then add the cooled melted butter in a slow steady stream, beating as it is added.

Spoon about 1 tablespoon batter into each madeleine shell, filling it about ¾ full.

Place in preheated oven and bake until golden brown, 12 to 15 minutes.

Remove cookies to cake rack and let cool, then dust with confectioner's sugar.

Makes 36 madeleines.

Langues de Chat
CATS' TONGUES

  5 tablespoons sweet butter
½ cup sugar
  1 tablespoon strained
    lemon juice
  1 teaspoon grated lemon rind
  4 egg whites
  1 cup cake flour

Grease baking sheets.

Preheat oven to 400°F.

Cream the butter until light and soft, then work in the sugar, lemon juice, and lemon rind until you have a creamy smooth mixture.

Add the egg whites 1 at a time, beating well after each addition. Fold in the flour.

Fit a pastry bag with a plain small tube, then fill about ⅔ full with the batter.

Press batter out onto prepared pans in strips about 2 inches long, leaving 1 inch between to allow for spreading.

Give the baking sheet a firm bang on the kitchen table to flatten the cookies.

Bake in preheated oven for 10 to 12 minutes, or until lightly browned.

Remove from cookie sheet to a cake rack to dry and cool completely, about 1 hour.

Pack in tightly covered tins for storing or giving. Cats' Tongues keep well.

Makes about 60.

Sand Tarts

1½ cups butter
1 cup sugar
3 egg whites
½ teaspoon almond extract
Pinch of salt
4 cups flour

Cream the butter with the sugar until very light and fluffy. Beat in the egg whites. Add flavoring and salt. Blend well, then add the flour 1 cup at a time, beating after each addition.

Shape the dough into 2 balls, place in the refrigerator, chill for 1 or more hours.

Preheat oven to 375°F.

Lightly grease cookie sheets.

Roll out 1 ball of dough at a time to about ⅛ inch thickness. Cut with small cookie cutter into any desired shape or use a sharp knife to cut into 1-x-1½-inch strips.

Bake on lightly greased cookie sheets in preheated oven for 8 to 10 minutes, or until edges of cookies are lightly browned.

Makes about 6 dozen small cookies.

Almond Fingers

½ cup (¼ pound) butter
¼ pound commercial canned
    almond paste
½ cup sugar
2 egg yolks, lightly beaten
½ teaspoon lemon extract
1 cup cake flour plus more
    as needed

Cream the butter with the almond paste and sugar until well blended. Beat in the egg yolks and lemon extract.

Add the flour and blend with a wooden spoon to a stiff dough that will leave the sides of the bowl and can be brought together in a ball.

Refrigerate for 1 hour.

Preheat oven to 400°F.

Roll out dough on a lightly floured board and cut with a sharp knife into strips about 1 inch long and ½ inch wide. Place strips on ungreased baking sheet and bake in preheated oven for 8 to 10 minutes, or until cookies are firm and golden in color.

Cool on a cake rack before packing or storing.

Makes about 3 dozen fingers.

To Speak
of Candy

"Sugar is sweet
and so are you."

I hope you are old enough to remember how marvelous
candy boxes used to be, decorated with bon mots like
the one above, with lace paper, photographs of sweet-
hearts (in full color), cupids, flowers, etc. You can
still find these old boxes in antique shops and they are
fun to collect if you are a devoted candy-maker.

The recipes here, like the boxes, are all old
favorites, the candy classics as it were, the tried and
true—fudge, divinity, fruit and nut rolls—the easy
fun-to-make candies that everyone loves. They cannot
be bought at any price; they have to be homemade.

It's hard to imagine someone not liking a gift of
homemade candy. Again suiting the type to the
recipient, small children and sophisticated adults
strangely enough like the same candies—popcorn
balls, candy canes, and peanut brittle—while teenagers

adore fudge, divinity, all the creamy rich kinds, preferably loaded with nuts. Send fruit and nut rolls to people who take food seriously and are always telling you about the new health food store they have discovered and to friends who consider themselves gourmets; they will love it.

Homemade candy is one of life's small pleasures. Wouldn't it be nice to receive a big box of small pleasures right now?

All About Equipment

Really good homemade candy is relatively easy to make, but like everything else there are tricks to the trade. The recipes included here are all long-time favorites. Simple and easy to follow, they require very little in the way of special equipment. Here's all you will need:

Large round-bottomed pot with a good sturdy handle
Long-handled wooden mixing spoon
Set of measuring spoons
Glass measuring cup
Candy thermometer
Long-handled fork
Cheese cloth
Chopping knife and board
Shallow oblong pans (preferably glass)

Special Tips

Generally speaking, candy should be made on a cool clear day; hot humid weather can cause candies to become sticky or sugary.

Grease the candy pot with butter before starting. This keeps the candy from boiling over.

Make sure your pot is large enough; it should hold at least four times the amount of your ingredients. In other words, if your ingredients total 4 cups, you need a 4-quart pot.

Creamy candies such as fudge should not be stirred after they reach the boiling point, and they must be allowed to cool to lukewarm before beating.

If crystals form on the sides of the pan while the candy is cooking, wipe them off with a long-handled fork, the tines of which are wrapped in wet cheese cloth.

Check the candy frequently with a candy thermometer. Do not allow the thermometer to touch the bottom or the sides of the pan as these surfaces are hotter than the liquid.

Check your thermometer for accuracy before starting by immersing it in boiling water. It should read 210°F.

You can check for doneness without a thermometer by using the cold water method. Fill a cup with cold water and drop a little of the hot liquid into it.

THERMOMETER	COLD WATER TEST
230°–234°F.	forms a flexible thread
234°–238°F.	forms a soft ball
238°–248°F.	forms a firm ball
248°–265°F.	forms a hard ball
265°–290°F.	forms a brittle ball (crack stage)

Finally, don't make candy when you are in a bad mood; candy-making is supposed to be fun.

Old-Fashioned Peanut Brittle

3 cups sugar
2/3 cup water
2/3 cup vinegar
1 cup light corn syrup
4 cups shelled peanuts
1 tablespoon butter, room
   temperature
2 teaspoons soda

Generously grease two baking sheets with butter.

Combine sugar, water, vinegar, and syrup in a large sauce pan and stir over moderate heat until sugar dissolves. Add peanuts and let boil to crack stage (270°–290°F. on candy thermometer). Remove from heat. Add butter and soda, stir quickly to blend. Pour out onto prepared baking sheets.

When cool, break into pieces. Makes about 2 pounds.

Creamy Chocolate Nut Fudge

5 squares unsweetened
   chocolate
1½ cups milk
4 cups sugar
⅛ teaspoon salt
¼ pound butter, room
   temperature
1 teaspoon vanilla, or
1 tablespoon grated
   orange rind
2 cups coarsely chopped
   walnuts or pecans

151

Melt the chocolate in the milk in a large heavy saucepan over low heat. Blend well. Add sugar and salt. Cook, stirring, over medium heat until sugar has dissolved, and mixture begins to boil. Then cook without stirring to 234°F. on your candy thermometer, or until a little of the mixture dropped into cold water will form a soft ball. Remove from heat.

Add butter and vanilla; do not stir. Just push the butter down into the hot fudge. Let stand at room temperature until thermometer drops to 110°F., or to lukewarm (without a thermometer use the old-fashioned finger test; it should be just warm to the touch). This cooling takes about 1 to 1½ hours, but do wait—it's the secret of really creamy thick candy.

Butter generously 2 8-x-4-x-3-inch loaf pans.

Beat lukewarm mixture until it begins to thicken and lose its gloss. Quickly fold in nuts. Pour immediately into prepared pans and let stand at room temperature 2 to 3 hours before cutting into squares.

Makes about 5 pounds, 68 to 70 generous pieces.

Divine Almond Divinity

    1 cup finely ground almonds
    2 egg whites
   ½ cup light corn syrup
  2½ cups sugar
   ¼ teaspoon salt
   ½ cup water
    2 drops almond extract
   ½ cup chopped almonds

Spread ground almonds out on waxed paper.

Place egg whites in a large bowl and bring to room temperature.

Combine corn syrup, sugar, salt, and water in a saucepan. Place over medium heat and stir until sugar has dissolved. Let cook without stirring to 262°F. on candy thermometer, or until a small amount of syrup will form a hard ball when dropped into a cup of cold water.

While syrup cooks, beat egg whites with a wire whisk until stiff enough to stand in firm peaks.

Prop the bowl with a folded kitchen towel or paper toweling a little to one side, then pour the syrup slowly over the beaten egg whites, beating constantly. Beat until mixture holds its shape and begins to dull.

Fold in almond extract and chopped almonds.

Drop mixture from tip of a teaspoon into ground almonds and roll to shape into balls.

Place balls not touching on a long platter or baking sheet and let stand at room temperature about 2 hours before packing into boxes.

Makes about 6 dozen pieces.

Turkish Delight

1 large orange
3 envelopes unflavored gelatin
2 cups sugar
1 cup boiling water
Red or green food coloring
Confectioner's sugar

Grate the peel from the orange, grating only the colored top peel. Squeeze the juice and reserve. Combine gelatin, sugar, and grated peel in a saucepan.

Pour in the boiling water. Place over low heat and stir until sugar and gelatin have dissolved. Let simmer, stirring often, for 20 minutes.

Remove from heat, add orange juice and tint pale red or green with 1 or 2 drops of food coloring.

Strain through a fine sieve into a shallow square or oblong aluminum baking dish to a depth of no more than 1 inch. Refrigerate until firm.

Turn out onto a wooden chopping board that you have spread first with confectioner's sugar. Cut into squares and roll each square in confectioner's sugar.

Store in a cool dry place.

Makes about 2 dozen pieces.

French Walnut Creams

8 squares semisweet chocolate
1 cup confectioner's sugar
1 tablespoon rum
1 well-beaten egg, room
    temperature
2 cups finely chopped walnuts

Heat chocolate in a double boiler over hot water until partly melted. Remove pan from water and stir rapidly until chocolate is entirely melted. Add sugar, rum, and egg. Beat until well blended. Refrigerate until firm enough to shape.

Form into small ½-inch balls.

Spread nuts out on waxed paper. Roll each ball in nuts and place not touching on foil. Let stand 1 hour.

154

Place each ball in a small fluted paper cup or wrap loosely in foil, before arranging in boxes.

Makes about 4 dozen pieces.

Chocolate Almond Figs

36 large dried figs
Boiling water
1 8-ounce jar unsalted dry
   roasted almonds
1 6-ounce package semisweet
   chocolate chips
1 tablespoon brandy
Confectioner's sugar

Place figs in a large bowl and add boiling water to cover. Let stand for 30 minutes. Drain and blot dry with paper toweling.

Preheat oven to 350°F.

Pulverize first almonds, then chocolate in electric blender or put through Mouli grater. Place in a mixing bowl and add brandy. Pound and mix to a stiff paste.

Use your kitchen shears to cut the stems from the figs. Then with your finger or the handle of a small spoon, make a deep depression in each at the stem ends.

Force about a teaspoon of the almond-chocolate mixture into each fig, packing it in tightly, and force openings closed. Place stuffed side up on a baking sheet and bake in preheated oven for 15 minutes.

Let cool to room temperature, then roll in confectioner's sugar.

Pack in airtight container.

Makes 36 pieces.

New Orleans Pralines

4 cups sugar
1 cup cream
1 teaspoon salt
6 cups chopped pecans

Butter cookie sheet.

Place 3 cups of the sugar and the cream in a preserving pot or in your largest saucepan. Stir over moderate heat until sugar is dissolved, then let simmer to soft ball stage, 238°F. on a candy thermometer.

Cook the remaining sugar in an enamelized cast-iron skillet over medium heat. Stir frequently until dissolved to a light brown syrup. Pour into cream and sugar mixture. Remove from heat and beat for a few seconds. Add salt. Beat until very thick and creamy; quickly fold in nuts. Drop by spoonfuls onto prepared cookie sheet.

Makes about 3 dozen pralines.

Christmas Popcorn Balls

½ cup brown sugar
½ cup white sugar
½ cup water
2 tablespoons light corn syrup
1 tablespoon butter, room temperature
6 cups popcorn
1 cup red cinnamon candy drops

156

Combine sugars, water, and corn syrup in a large saucepan. Stir over medium heat until sugar has dissolved. Cook, without stirring, to soft ball stage (238°F. on your candy thermometer). Remove from heat and add butter. Stir only until butter has dissolved. Cool slightly. Put the popcorn and cinnamon candy in a bowl large enough to allow for thorough mixing.

Pour the syrup slowly over the popcorn and candy. Mix well with 2 forks. Moisten your hands with cold water and shape mixture into balls.

Wrap each in plastic wrap and tie with green ribbon or string.

Makes about 12 balls.

Drunken Turtles

1 pound soft caramels
2 tablespoons sweet butter
2 tablespoons cognac, or other
  good brandy
2 cups pecan halves
8 ounces bittersweet chocolate

Melt caramels in butter and cognac or brandy in top of double boiler over simmering water. Remove from heat and let stand for 10 minutes.

Place pecan halves on waxed paper in groups of 4, 3 close together and 1 on top.

Spoon caramel mixture over center of nuts. Don't cover tips. Let stand for about 30 minutes, or until set.

Melt chocolate in top of double boiler over simmering water until partially melted. Remove from heat and stir until completely melted. Then cool to lukewarm.

Spread cooled chocolate over caramels with small coffee spoon.

Makes about 3½ dozen turtles.

Apricot Bars

1 pound dried apricots
2 cups boiling water
1 large orange
4 pieces preserved ginger
2 cups sugar
Confectioner's sugar

Place apricots in a large bowl and cover with the boiling water. Let stand for about 2 hours. Drain.

Cut orange into quarters and remove seeds. Put through a food grinder, retaining all the juices. Grind ginger.

Combine apricots, orange and ginger in a saucepan and stir over moderate heat until sugar has dissolved. Let simmer, stirring constantly until mixture is very thick, about 5 minutes. Spread out onto a lightly buttered baking sheet. Let stand until cool and firm. Cut into bars. Roll each bar in powdered sugar. Place on cake rack to dry before packing.

Makes about 24 bars.

Fruit and Nut Bars

½ pound raisins
¼ pound figs
¼ pound dates
¼ pound candied orange peel
2 pounds chopped walnuts
2 tablespoons chopped
    (preserved in syrup) ginger
Confectioner's sugar

Mix together fruits, walnuts, and ginger. Put through the fine blade of grinder or use a very sharp serrated knife to chop as finely as possible.

Turn out onto a wooden chopping board that you have "floured" with confectioner's sugar. Knead, then press out about ½ inch thick. Cut into small bars.

Pack in layers between sheets of waxed paper.

Makes about 4 pounds candy.

Christmas Candy Canes

3 cups sugar
¾ cup light corn syrup
¾ cup water
1 tablespoon grated lemon rind
2 tablespoons lemon juice
1½ teaspoons peppermint extract
Red food coloring

Butter 2 large platters generously.

Place all ingredients except peppermint extract and food coloring into an enamel or glass saucepan and bring to a boil. Cook without stirring until candy reaches the soft crack stage (285°F. on a candy thermometer). Stir in peppermint extract. Pour half of the candy on one of the platters, add a few drops red food coloring to remaining candy and pour on second platter. When cool enough to handle, pull and roll separately into sticks. Twist one around the other and bend one end to form a handle. Allow to harden, then wrap in cellophane. Store in a dry place.

Makes about 3 dozen canes.

This and That

This is a collection of personal favorites that I enjoy making and giving. They range from a steamed date nut bread to a quick and easy herb vinegar and a sweet-scented potpourri that is no less welcome for being simple to make.

You can add greatly to your "This and That" favorites by shopping for interesting containers—good-looking simple crocks for cheese spreads, charming ceramic and glass bottles for your vinegars, jars and bowls to hold potpourri. I like to find old containers in antique and thrift shops, but the gift department of your local department store probably has a good selection if you choose with care. Generally speaking, it's best to keep things simple, as that way it will fit in with the decor of the recipient's house. For example, potpourri jars and bowls are usually on display, so unless you are very sure of your friends' tastes it is better to stay with plain colors and simple shapes.

For some reason Chinese design seems to fit into everyone's decorating scheme. I use replicas of Chinese ginger jars and rice bowls that come in good solid colors like clear blue, yellow, and lacquer red. For cheese spreads and nut butters old-fashioned plain stoneware crocks are the best choice. I cover the top snugly with foil and tie a big fat bow around the crock. Cork-stoppered cruets are best for vinegars. They are both decorative and useful. You can buy beautiful new ones in plain crystal that have great style, or interesting ceramic and glass ones are often to be found in antique shops. However, if you want to be thrifty save any pretty wine bottles that come

your way; they make very attractive containers for vinegars.

There should be something for everyone on your list in this chapter: cheese spreads and nut butters for your cocktail party group, puddings and mincemeat for family presents, herb vinegars for dieters to dress up their calorie-conscious green salad, as well as pickles and relishes for "that man," and a fragrant potpourri for the woman who has everything.

Best of all, easy or elaborate, these are very special gifts from you, gifts with a very personal touch that makes all the difference in the world to the recipient, a difference that cannot be bought at any price.

New England Summer Mincemeat

For the most luscious pies ever!

12 tart cooking apples
18 large green tomatoes
 1 cup dark molasses
½ cup dark rum
 3 cups light brown sugar
½ teaspoon salt
 1 pound seedless dark raisins
 1 teaspoon cinnamon
 1 teaspoon ginger
 1 teaspoon allspice
 1 cup vinegar

Wash the apples, remove the blossom ends, and core but do not peel them. Wash the tomatoes.

Put apples and tomatoes through the coarse blade

of your food chopper or chop very fine. Combine in a large preserving kettle and add the remaining ingredients. Stir over moderate heat until sugar has dissolved, then increase heat to very high and boil hard until quite thick, 10 to 15 minutes.

Immediately ladle into clean hot jars and seal. Makes about 4 quarts.

Old-Fashioned Bread and Butter Pickles

10 small cucumbers
 1 large purple onion
 2 small hot red peppers
½ cup salt
 2 quarts ice cubes
 2 quarts water, chilled in refrigerator
 3 cups cider vinegar
 1 cup light brown sugar
 2 cups white sugar
 1 tablespoon mustard seed
 1 tablespoon celery seed
 1 teaspoon turmeric

Buy small firm unwaxed cucumbers of uniform size. Cut into slices about ⅛ inch thick.

Peel and coarse-chop onion. Chop fine the red peppers. Place vegetables in a large non-metal bowl or earthenware crock and add salt. Stir and toss to distribute salt evenly. Add ice cubes and again toss and stir until distributed with vegetables. Add chilled water to 1 inch of brim of bowl or crock. Refrigerate for 3 to 4 hours. Stir occasionally. Drain.

Combine remaining ingredients in a large enamel preserving pot. Stir over medium heat until sugar has dissolved, then bring to a boil. Add drained vegetables and again bring to a boil. Lower heat and let simmer for about 10 minutes. Remove pot from heat and, using a large slotted spoon, transfer vegetables to hot, very clean jars.

Bring syrup to a boil, then ladle over vegetables to ¼ inch of rim of jars. With a scalded knife break up any air bubbles in syrup. Then immediately seal the jars.

Makes about 6 pints.

Pickled Carrot Sticks

4 bunches firm, fresh
  medium-sized carrots
3 cups white vinegar
3 cups sugar
1 tablespoon pickling spices
1 teaspoon mustard seed
2 sticks cinnamon
1 tablespoon ground ginger

For best flavor use fresh not storage carrots.

Scrape carrots and cut them into sticks about ¼ inch thick and 3¼ inches long. Cover with water and bring to a boil. Let simmer for about 10 minutes, or until they just begin to become tender. Drain.

Combine vinegar and sugar in a large enamel pot, and stir over medium heat until sugar has dissolved, then let simmer gently over low heat.

Tie pickling spices and mustard seed in a small cheesecloth bag and add to simmering syrup. Stir in ginger and let cook for 30 minutes. Add carrot sticks and remove pot from heat.

Let cool to room temperature, then cover and let stand overnight. (May be kept in your refrigerator.) Next morning reheat slowly, then bring to a boil. Lower heat and let simmer for ten minutes. Remove and discard spice bag. Remove pot from heat.

Using a slotted spoon, transfer carrot sticks to half-pint straight-sided mason jars, packing them upright and close together in the jars.

Bring syrup to a full boil and pour over carrot sticks to ¼ of inch of rim of jars, covering sticks completely with syrup. Seal at once.

Makes about 6 half-pint jars.

Indian Summer Relish

    6 medium-size green peppers,
      seeded
    6 medium-size sweet red peppers
    3 small green chili peppers
    2 large mild purple onions, peeled
    3 cups cider vinegar
  ¾ cup brown sugar,
      packed down
  ¼ teaspoon mustard seed
    1 tablespoon salt
    2 teaspoons freshly ground
      black pepper
    2 cups fresh corn kernels

Put peppers and onions through largest blade of meat grinder.

Combine vinegar, sugar, mustard seed, salt, and pepper in preserving kettle over medium heat, and stir until sugar dissolves.

Bring to a full boil, then lower heat and let simmer for 10 minutes. Add ground peppers and onions and simmer for another 10 minutes. Add corn kernels and let cook a final 5 minutes.

Ladle into clean hot jars and seal.

Makes about 4 pints.

English Lemon Butter

3 large lemons
2½ cups honey
½ bottle (3 ounces)
    liquid pectin

Grate rind from one lemon. Squeeze and strain lemon juice.

Combine lemon rind, lemon juice, and honey in a large, deep saucepan. Stir over moderate heat until mixture reaches a full boil. Remove from heat and stir in pectin. Again bring to a full boil but this time over high heat. Boil hard for 1 minute, stirring constantly. Remove from heat and stir for a full 3 minutes. This last step will give you the smooth, creamy consistency that makes this butter such a treat on muffins or as a filling for sponge-cake layers or a jelly roll.

Ladle into clean hot jars. Seal with paraffin.

Makes about 4 half-pint jars.

Cantaloupe Butter

6 cups pureed ripe cantaloupe
    (about 2 medium)
2 cups orange sections
1 tablespoon grated lime rind
½ cup lime juice
5 cups sugar
2 cinnamon sticks

To puree cantaloupe, remove peel and cut into pieces; puree in electric blender (half a melon at a time) or food mill. Combine in large heavy kettle with remaining ingredients. Place over moderate heat and bring slowly to a boil, stirring frequently. Reduce heat; cook over moderately low heat for 1½ to 1¾ hours, or until thick, stirring frequently. (When cold, the butter is almost the same consistency as when it is hot; it does not thicken on standing the way most jams do.) Remove from heat. Remove cinnamon sticks and ladle immediately into clean hot jars and seal.

Makes 5 half-pint jars.

Spiced Vinegar

2¼ quarts white vinegar

½ cup sugar

2 cloves garlic, peeled and minced

2 tablespoons mixed pickling spices

1 small (approximately 1-x-1-inch) square fresh ginger, crushed

2 teaspoons salt

Place all ingredients in a large enamelized cast-iron pot. Bring to a full boil, then reduce heat and let simmer for 30 minutes. Remove from heat and let stand at room temperature until cold. Strain through a fine sieve which you have lined with cheesecloth.

Bottle and cork.

Makes 4 pint bottles.

Tarragon Vinegar

3 tablespoons chopped fresh
tarragon leaves
2 cloves garlic, peeled and
cut in half lengthwise
1 quart white wine vinegar
1 pint red wine vinegar

Crush the tarragon leaves lightly with a wooden mallet
to bruise them slightly and place in a non-metal
crock or glass jar and add the garlic.

Heat the white wine vinegar to just below boiling
point, and pour it over herbs. Cover and let stand in
a warm place for 24 hours. Remove and discard the
garlic. Let stand covered for 2 weeks. Strain through
a fine sieve that you have lined with cheesecloth.

Add the red wine vinegar. Bottle and cork.
Makes 3 pints.

Hot Chili Vinegar

8 small hot red peppers
3 cups white wine vinegar

Chop peppers and put them in a 1-quart mason jar;
add the vinegar. Seal. Shake the jar every other day
for 2 weeks. Then strain, bottle, and seal.
Makes 3 half-pints.

Garlicky Wine Vinegar

1 bottle (4/5 quart) inexpensive
   but good red wine
2 pints cider vinegar
4 cloves garlic, peeled and
   split lengthwise

Combine ingredients in an enamel pot. Bring to boiling point but do not allow to boil hard. Let simmer very gently for about 15 minutes. Remove from heat and let stand until cool.

Strain through cheesecloth. Refrigerate overnight, then strain once more. Pour into clean bottles and seal.

Makes about 8 half-pints.

English Potted Cheese

1 pound aged sharp cheddar
   cheese
¼ pound sweet butter, room
   temperature
¼ teaspoon dry mustard
Dash of Worcestershire sauce
1 cup chopped walnuts
½ cup dry sherry

Grate the cheese into a mixing bowl. Add remaining ingredients and beat with a wooden spoon until very smooth.

Pack into 1 or 2 small earthenware crocks. Press a circle of waxed paper directly over the cheese then cover with lid or foil.

Store in refrigerator for 24 hours before using. Will keep refrigerated 2 to 3 weeks.

Makes 2 cups.

Mexican Cheese Crock

6 or 8 small hot chili peppers, finely chopped

2 small white onions, peeled and chopped

1 clove garlic, peeled and split lengthwise in half

3 tablespoons butter

2 cups canned tomatoes

¼ teaspoon salt

¼ teaspoon freshly ground black pepper

2 pounds Monterey Jack cheese, or semisharp cheddar cheese

2 to 3 dashes Worcestershire sauce

Salt to taste

Sauté chili peppers, onion, and garlic in butter over moderate heat until onion is limp. Add tomatoes, salt, and pepper. Let simmer over low heat for 25 to 30 minutes. Remove from heat. Fish out and discard garlic. Let cool to lukewarm before using.

Grate cheese into a mixing bowl. Add cooled chili sauce and Worcestershire sauce. Blend with a wooden spoon. Taste and add additional salt if desired.

Pack into 3 or 4 small crocks. Cover cheese directly with waxed paper before covering with lid or foil.

Refrigerate for 24 hours before using. Will keep 2 to 3 weeks stored in refrigerator.

Makes about 4 cups.

Blue-Cheese Spread

½ pound blue cheese
½ pound cream cheese
2 tablespoons chives
½ cup finely chopped
  blanched almonds
Dash Tabasco sauce
¼ cup cognac, or good
  quality brandy

Bring all ingredients to room temperature. Combine in mixing bowl and beat with a fork or an electric blender until well blended. Pack into crocks. Let ripen in refrigerator for 24 hours.

Store in refrigerator.

Makes about 2 cups.

Curried Cashew Butter

2 cups unsalted cashew nuts
½ to ¾ cup vegetable oil
½ teaspoon sugar
1 teaspoon curry powder
Salt to taste
Paprika

Combine ½ cup of the nuts, 2 tablespoons of the oil, the sugar, and curry powder in the container of an electric blender. Blend at high speed, stopping when necessary to scrape down the sides of the container until the mixture is smooth but still a little grainy.

Add additional oil if mixture becomes too dry to blend.

Scrape butter out into a large bowl then puree remaining nuts with oil in the same manner.

When all the nuts have been pureed, season with salt to taste.

Pack into 1 or 2 small earthenware crocks or small bowls. Sprinkle surface lightly with paprika. Cover with foil and store in refrigerator. Butter will keep for 2 to 3 weeks.

Makes about 3 half-pint jars.

Gourmet Peanut Butter

2 cups unsalted dry roasted
   peanuts
½ to ¾ cup vegetable oil
2 or 3 dashes Tabasco sauce
Salt to taste
Paprika

Follow directions for making Curried Cashew Butter.

174

Sesame Walnut Butter

2 cups unsalted walnuts
2 tablespoons sesame oil
½ to ¾ cup vegetable oil
Salt to taste

Follow directions for making Curried Cashew Butter.

Chestnut Jam

From France a jam to serve with venison, game birds, roasted meats, or—and more often at our house —with thick slices of crusty French bread that has been spread with sweet country butter. I can think of nothing I like better to serve with a freshly made pot of steaming hot Jamaican coffee.

2 pounds chestnuts
1 pound sugar
2 cups water
1- to 2-inch length of vanilla bean

With a sharp little knife cut a cross in the flat side of each chestnut. Put them in a saucepan, cover with water, and bring to a boil. Lower heat and let simmer for about 15 minutes. Drain, cover with cold water, and drain again.

While the chestnuts are still warm, remove the shells and peel off the brown skins. Puree them in a food mill or through a sieve.

Combine the sugar, 1 cup of the water, and the

175

vanilla bean in a preserving pot. Place over medium heat, bring to a boil, and let boil for about 15 minutes. Stir often and skim off the foam as it rises to the surface.

Moisten the chestnut puree with the remaining water and blend to a paste. Stir this into the boiling syrup. Let cook—very gently now—for about 20 minutes or until the jam is as thick as you want it to be. Ladle into clean hot jars and seal. I'm told this jam keeps well, but for once I'm unable to guarantee it because my own chestnut jam is always eaten the week it is made.

Makes about 4 half-pints.

Paté Maison

    1 pound braunschweiger
       (smoked liverwurst)
 ½ pound (2 sticks) butter
 ¼ cup cognac, or good
       quality brandy
 ½ cup chutney (homemade or
       Major Gray variety), very
       finely chopped
Dash Tabasco sauce
Salt to taste
Chopped blanched and toasted
    almonds, optional
Paprika

Bring liverwurst and butter to room temperature. Combine in a mixing bowl. Add cognac or brandy and cream until well blended and smooth. Blend in chutney. Season with Tabasco and salt to taste.

Pack into small crocks and if desired cover surface with chopped almonds and sprinkle with paprika.

Or, chill mixture until firm enough to roll into 2 small logs. Roll in chopped almonds and dust with paprika.

Store in refrigerator.

Should be made 1 or 2 days before giving or using so that flavors can mellow. Stored in refrigerator will keep 7 to 8 days.

Enough to fill 3 small (8 ounce) crocks or make 2 logs.

Melba Sauce

I know of no more elegant way to end a party dinner menu than with melba sauce over plain vanilla ice cream—unless it's with peach melba, that classic dessert. But the last time I bought an 8-ounce bottle of melba sauce at my local gourmet food shop, it cost only a few cents under a dollar. After that I made twice that quantity at home for about fifty cents, and it tasted even better than the "store bought" kind.

Because of this—even though a sauce doesn't rightly belong in this book—it's included.

 2 10-ounce packages frozen
   raspberries
 ½ cup water
1½ cups sugar
 3 tablespoons strained fresh
   lemon juice

Unwrap frozen berries and place them in a large bowl. Let thaw at room temperature.

Place thawed berries and water in a preserving kettle and bring to boil over medium heat. Crush the berries with a wooden spoon to bring out the juice. When quite liquid (1 or 2 minutes), pour the berries through a fine sieve set over a large bowl. Crush with back of a spoon to extract as much juice as possible.

Combine the strained juice with the sugar and lemon juice in the preserving kettle and bring to a boil over high heat. Cook, stirring constantly, until mixture thickens to quite "syrupy." Pour into clean hot jars and seal.

Makes 2 half-pint jars.

Back Bay Steamed Date Nut Bread

Save 2 coffee cans for this one.

2 cups whole wheat pastry
  flour (available at health food
  stores), or substitute
  all-purpose flour
2 cups yellow cornmeal
2 teaspoons baking soda
1 teaspoon salt
3/4 cup finely chopped dates
3/4 cup chopped walnuts
2 cups buttermilk
2/3 cup milk
3/4 cup dark molasses

Grease 2 (1 pound) coffee cans generously with vegetable shortening.

Sift flour, cornmeal, soda, and salt into a large mixing bowl and blend well. Stir in dates and nuts.

In a smaller bowl combine buttermilk, milk, and dark molasses.

Add milk mixture to flour mixture about ½ cup at a time, blending with a wooden spoon after each addition.

Ladle mixture into greased coffee cans, filling each about ⅔ full. Place pieces of heavy aluminum foil over each can and hold firmly in place with rubber bands or tie down with heavy-duty string.

Place cans on a rack in a deep heavy pot. Add boiling water to come a little more than halfway up sides of cans. Cover pot.

Let bread steam 2½ to 3 hours over medium heat so that water stays at a simmering point just below boiling. Add more water to pot as needed to maintain level around cans.

Remove cans to a wire rack to cool.

For gift-giving, cool bread in cans. Then wrap cans in foil and store in refrigerator until ready to gift wrap.

Makes 2 loaves.

Note: Tie a note to each can with instructions for reheating.

To Reheat: Unwrap and place covered cans on a rack in boiling water in a large pot. Steam for about 30 minutes, or until heated through.

Potpourri

This *is* a preserve, even though you can't eat it. It's fun to make, to give, or to keep for yourself, so I think it merits inclusion in this book. Rugosa roses make the best potpourri. They are the most fragrant and their petals keep their bright color for the longest time—or so it seems to me—but any fragrant variety of rose will do. Just let your nose be the judge.

Gather the petals midmorning on a sunny day when the dew is off them. If you have lemon verbena, rose geraniums, or syringa blossoms, use their petals too, but you should have about 4 times as many rose petals as of the others. Spread them out on old newspapers in a dry place. If you have a work table in a tool shed, that's perfect. If not, any place away from drafts and out of your way for 1 to 2 weeks will do.

Once your petals are dry—really dry—you are ready to begin.

8 to 10 cups dried rose petals,
   or 6 cups rose petals mixed
   with 1 cup lemon verbena
   petals and 1 cup rose
   geranium petals
Salt
24 whole cloves
6 sticks cinnamon, broken up
1 ounce orris root
8 drops oil of rose
4 drops oil of lavender
Peel from one large orange
   (orange part only)
Brandy

Put the dried petals in a large bowl and sprinkle lightly with salt. Toss the petals as you would a salad to distribute the salt evenly. Let stand in a dry place for 1 week, tossing the petals each day and adding a light sprinkling of salt each time you toss.

At the end of this time add the spices and toss again to blend. Cover the bowl with foil and let stand 1 more day. Then add the orris root and blend well.

Cut the orange rind into the thinnest possible slivers, about ½ inch long, and gently stir this into the potpourri.

Fill small jars or crocks with the mixture. Sprinkle a little brandy over the surface of each. Cover the jars with tight-fitting lids. This particular mixture lasts and lasts and lasts. The batch I made 5 years ago is still fragrant.

Index

183

185